NOW
That They Are
GROWN

*I have looked forward to Ron Greer's latest offering with great antici-
pation, and* Now That They Are Grown *exceeds all of my expectations.
Ron is a wise and helpful guide for parents looking for a mature, healthy
relationship with their adult children. His writing comes across as a
long-trusted friend who is passing along valuable wisdom gleaned from
years of experience gained while walking this road with others. Ron's
words not only educate, but they also encourage parents that they can do
this!* Now That They Are Grown *is a job well done!*
—Dr. Bill Britt, Senior Minister, Peachtree Road United Methodist
Church

*A prominent college coach was recently asked if players had changed in
the last few years. His answer would not have surprised Ron Greer.
"Naw," he emphatically stated in his southern twang. "The kids are the
same. They just want to play. But the parents have lost their minds!" Ron
may not be quite that critical, but he knows most of us need help in dealing with our adult children when they are busy flying the coop. He has
written a wonderful guide for parents who have maintained their sanity
but simply do not know what to do. Enjoy Ron's stories, but mostly take
note of his wisdom. I know it will change your life, it may change your
children's lives, and it might even help the grandchildren!*
—Bill Curry, Georgia State University head football coach and the
author of *Ten Men You Meet in the Huddle: Lessons from a Football Life*

Ron has shared (his) wisdom in Now That They Are Grown:
Successfully Parenting Your Adult Children. *This book is an easy read;
is chock-full of wisdom; and is sensitively, caringly, creatively com-
posed. This pastoral counselor knows the dynamics of parenting adult
children in this contemporary context. He advocates mutual respect and
magnanimous good will between the generations both in "letting them
go" and in "negotiating a new adult-to-adult relationship."*
—Dr. Jap Keith, Southeast Regional Director of the Association for
Clinical Pastoral Education, Inc., Professor Emeritus of
Pastoral Care and Counseling of Columbia Theological
Seminary, American Association of Pastoral Counselors

Ronald J.Greer

NOW

That They Are

GROWN

*Successfully
Parenting
Your Adult
Children*

Abingdon Press
Nashville

Now That They Are Grown
Successfully Parenting Your Adult Children

This book is printed on acid-free paper.

Library of Congress Cataloging-in-Publication Data

ISBN 978-1-4267-4191-3
Cataloging in Publication Data has been applied for with the Library of Congress.

Scripture quotations are from the New Revised Standard Version of the Bible, copyrighted 1989, by the Division of Christian Education of the National Council of the Churches of Christ in the United States of America. Used by permission.

12 13 14 15 16 17 18 19 20 21—10 9 8 7 6 5 4 3 2 1

MANUFACTURED IN THE UNITED STATES OF AMERICA

To Karen

*my dear partner in this experience
of being the parents
of two wonderful adults*

For everything there is a season,
and a time for every matter under heaven:
a time to be born, and a time to die;
a time to plant, and a time to pluck up what is planted; . . .
a time to embrace, and a time to refrain from embracing.
—Ecclesiastes 3:1-2, 5b

Contents

Prologue

WE HAD JUST MET, but quickly the conversation turned to the recent marriage of her son. This delightful woman explained he was her youngest child, the last to be married. The mother of the groom was still aglow over the wedding and told me all about it.

I remember nothing of the wedding details. Yet I remember vividly her description of the events that followed.

After the wedding reception, her husband dropped her off at their home and left to run an errand. She said she went inside alone and made herself a cup of coffee. She took it into the den, slipped off her shoes, propped her feet up on the ottoman, and for the next fifteen minutes just sat there reliving the glorious wedding that had just taken place.

Finishing her coffee, she took the cup back to the kitchen and started down the hall to change out of her elegant dress. She said she got halfway down the hall, to the doorway of the bedroom of her son who had just married. She described it as if a magnet had pulled her into his room. She looked around. There on the wall were his posters and his banners. There on his chest of drawers were his trophies and the picture of his sweetheart who was now his bride. And there on the floor, at the foot of his bed, were two dirty socks.

She said, "I was all right until I got to the socks. But I knew it was the last pair of his dirty socks I'd ever pick up again." The tears came to her eyes as she told it, just as the tears had come to her eyes as she had lived it. With tissue now in hand, she described how she ran down the hall, threw herself on her bed, and had the cry she needed to have.

Her life had changed. It had been, indeed, a day of celebration. But in the privacy of her heart, in the privacy of her home, she could feel the rest of the story. She would always be her sons' mama, but—having invested three decades in actively mothering—she was a seasoned veteran at a role that was no longer needed.

Life is filled with change. As our sons and daughters move into young adulthood, our roles as loving parents change dramatically. Now they are grown. It's time for changes. We will make the transition, though not always with the grace we would prefer.

The intent of this book is to help us avoid as many pitfalls as possible in making the change from parenting children to being parents of young adults. It's a challenge. It isn't easy. How do we nurture our adult children while encouraging their independence and maturity? Where is the balance? How do we respond to them in times of struggle? What is supportive, yet not intrusive? What is caring, yet not enabling dependency?

The questions are important. The answers are not obvious. It is a new day and a new relationship. The page has been turned, and we are now writing the new chapter in the life of our family. It is important that we get it right. It is important that we are true to the integrity of who we as parents and children are . . . now.

Letting Go

I think of the pages that follow as a conversation between you and me—fellow parents of adult sons and daughters— like my conversation with the mother of the groom. I imagine us, as friends, sitting on the deck of a cabin looking out over the mountains of western North Carolina. A group of us, now empty nesters, have gone up for a relaxing weekend. No agenda. Just hiking, talking, and doing nothing purposeful. It's early morning. You and I are the first two up. We are even ahead of the sun, though it's not far beneath the horizon. We see the silhouette of the Blue Ridge Mountains in the distance. Below us, in the valley, is a blanket of thick morning fog.

The air is chilly as we each settle comfortably into our rocking chairs, sipping our coffee and talking. We readily

solve the world's problems. Then the talk turns to family. I
see some concern on your face as you talk about your chil-
dren, and I begin asking questions. You seem relieved,
almost glad to be invited to talk about it.

You explain that there is no current crisis and that you
have wonderful children, but you are struggling with defin-
ing the new relationship with them. This new role seems to
be part parent, part friend, but when are you which? And
how? What is it supposed to look like? Sometimes they ask
your opinion—then at other times they seem to resent your
giving it. You are still trying to hit your stride.

You pause and mention you are a little embarrassed
even to be talking about it, especially with no crisis at
hand. But this is too puzzling and too important not to talk
it through.

So, with coffee in hand, let's talk.[1]

THE RELATIONSHIPS with our adult children can become truly
wonderful. But it takes real effort. It takes being intentional. Our
sons and daughters move from childhood to adulthood. We move
from being a parent to becoming a peer. It is a transition we may
navigate awkwardly, but ultimately it's a relationship we can successfully redefine.

From the moment of our children's births, when they were
totally reliant on us, we began a two-decade process from their
dependence to their independence, two decades of what was often
a turbulent ride. Infancy was followed by childhood, and then
came adolescence (God bless us all), with its disconnection, its

turmoil, and its breaking away. And one day this disconnection and turmoil subsided (thank you, Jesus) and transformed into a new chapter that we can embrace and enjoy the rest of our lives. This disconnection ends, when it all goes well, with the reconnection of a healthy, mutually respectful relationship as adults to adults. We don't cease to nurture. We don't cease being parents. We redefine parenthood based on our new peer-ship with our adult children.

But how on earth do we get there? Let's start with what I have come to see as the goals of parenting young adults.

GOALS OF PARENTING YOUNG ADULTS

There are four goals we will use as our focus as we parent young adults:

1. To help them move forward into this new chapter of their lives, with new directions, priorities, and loyalties.
2. To help them achieve their full maturity as adults, taking responsibility for their lives, making wise decisions, and living with integrity and character.
3. To establish a new, loving relationship with them—adult to adult—with mutual respect and appropriate boundaries.
4. To become more focused on this new chapter of our lives; with the nest now empty, we spread our wings, too, in new directions with new priorities.

I begin with these goals to serve as anchors, as touchstones to help with our focus and grounding. These goals are reference points to guide us in our thinking and our decisions as parents of young adults. The first two are about them:

To help them move forward into this new chapter of their lives.

To help them achieve their full maturity as adults.

The third involves our relationship with them:

To establish a new, loving relationship with them—adult to adult.

And in the fourth we shift our attention totally to ourselves:

To become more focused on this new chapter of our lives.

As I think of the importance of these touchstones, I remember hearing a story on National Public Radio. It was about a man named James Smith, who at forty-five learned he had early-onset Alzheimer's. He was articulate as he spoke with sadness of his emotional pain.

Then he talked of the abilities he still had. He still could drive around his hometown. Usually he could find his way if he were on familiar streets, but often he would get lost if he were in unfamiliar territory. He said, "The GPS is on my dash, and it's one that speaks to you. It has a button on it that says, 'Go Home.' Any time I find myself totally lost, all I have to do is touch that button."

Whenever he was lost he would hit "Go Home" on his GPS. It would take him home, and he would start over again.

This is how I think of these four goals—as our touchstones for when we get lost. They are for the times we lose our focus and begin parenting in ways that don't fit this new, current chapter. Somehow we know it doesn't fit. We may be treating them as the children they once were or as seasoned adults they are not yet. When we know it isn't working, we hit the "Go Home" button on our GPS, and it takes us back to our four touchstones . . . and we start over again.

THIS NEW CHAPTER

We have entered our new chapter with its empty—or at least emptying—nest. It can be delightful and fulfilling, while the relationships with our young adult children become personal and meaningful in a different way. (This is a good thing, since they are the ones who will one day be taking away our car keys and carting us off to some retirement community. We want that to be done by someone who loves us.)

When our first child, Patrick, was born, a pastoral counselor friend of Karen's and mine wrote us a letter. Here is a portion of it:

> But try to understand that this child is neither an extension of you nor a propagation of your personality. This child is a "new being," a unique person, and with your loving will develop his own personality. This unique child of God has a right to become who he is. It has been your privilege to participate in this act of creation, yet you had no power to determine what you were creating. What was embedded is now yet fully to emerge. What is now dormant will one day be realized. What

5

is now potential will be actualized, and this becoming needs only your loving support, not your molding. Your task is to accept this child for who he is—to be loving, to be caring, to be supportive, to provide resources, to nurture, to encourage, to educate, and, finally, to let go.[2]

"And, finally, to let go." We often hear and read that this new relationship with our adult children involves "letting go"; and, of course, it does. We let go of all kinds of parental responsibilities and duties. This "letting go" is a process—we are letting go, bit by bit, piece by piece, as the years go by. Our job descriptions get shorter. Our responsibilities as parents lessen. Then, as our children reach adulthood, when it goes well, we have worked ourselves out of a job. We relinquish the reins as we turn over to them the responsibility for their lives. We retire. Oh, we'll be called back into momentary service in those times of crisis or need for counsel, but largely we retire as active parents.

Jesus pointed to that same transition from the other vantage: ". . . a man shall leave his father and mother . . ." (Mark 10:7). The letting go works both ways. It's a big transition, a big change for us all.

It is time for them to move on, so we release them in order to give them the best chance of maturing into the adults they can become. We let go so they can grow. Many colleges formalize this on the day that incoming freshmen arrive. They will have either a "parting ceremony" or at least a designated time for parents to say good-bye to their eighteen-year-olds and leave the campus. This is a significant step in their development. We hand over the baton to them so they can grow into the adults they now are becoming, so they can run their own race.

Then we will reconnect with them in a new and meaningful way as one adult to another.

This letting go may go smoothly, as the natural transition from one phase of life to the next. Or it may be more difficult. Parents may struggle with moving on from the responsibilities of active parenthood. They may struggle with redefining how their lives now will look. Or their adult children may resist assuming those responsibilities for themselves, enjoying the freedoms of adulthood without claiming the maturity and duty that come with it. Yes, as we will discuss later, it can be difficult.

Some parents flinch at the phrase "letting go," since it implies less of a relationship. But it isn't. Although there is much less face-to-face time with your adult children, this is not the end of a relationship but the beginning of a new one. It is the ending of the previous chapter, of who they were, so that we might begin the next chapter and connect with who they are.

Two friends of mine learned I was writing this book on being parents of young adults. They are both mothers of fine young adults, and both have excellent relationships with them. In separate conversations, I received two rather different responses from them on the book's topic. One said, "Well, that's going to be a short book. Just tell them, 'Let 'em go.'" The other said something quite different, "You never really let them go, of course." Both are wise women and wonderful mothers. And both are right.

We move from one caring relationship to a different caring relationship—with new boundaries, with different ways of connecting, but with just as much love. With a healthy, mutual respect, parents and their adult daughters and sons can transition into being the best of friends.

In all of this "letting go," we do not cease to be our adult children's parents. They will always be in our awareness and in our hearts. We will always think of their welfare and be supportive in any way we can be. We do, indeed, become friends as fellow adults. Yet it is a unique friendship. They know we've got their back, as the cliché goes these days. We are there for them and always will be. That support will never change, no matter how much they mature or how old we become or how completely they may have outgrown us. But regardless of how much they grow, mature, or achieve, they know we are in the wings. We are there for them, supportively, lovingly. We remain their mothers and their fathers.

Columnist Ellen Goodman put it this way:

> What I did next—what we did next—was to reinvent our mother-daughter relationship again and again. We'd already gone from mother and toddler to mother and teenager—a transition that required the flexibility of a Bikram yoga instructor. Gradually, though, we were transformed from mother and college student to mother and mother, woman and woman. I changed from guide to confidante, from safety net to reality check.[3]

I always think of a mobile as the perfect metaphor for a family, a mobile with its delicate pieces hanging in balance from the thinnest lines of filament. Any significant change in the family—a birth or death, a marriage or divorce—and a piece is added or suddenly taken away. Our mobile sways from the sudden shift. It sways as we move from relating with them as children to connecting with them as young adults. It sways as our relationship is in transition, is being redefined. It is a time of uncertainty and some anxiety, for we don't know what this important relationship will look like when our mobile has achieved its new balance.

We live in the present. We look back to savor the memories, learn from the past, or work through any unfinished emotional business, but we live in the present moment. We believe that relationships with those whom we love will endure. They will endure change. They will endure the swinging of our familial mobile. We come out on the far side of these changes as somewhat new families with redefined relationships. We haven't tried to hang on to what used to be. We embrace what is. We are transformed. And it is good.

2

Today's Young Adults

Are you ready for a refill on the coffee?

The time flies. It's now well past sunup. We hear stirring inside as others begin to rally. We watch as the sun begins to burn off the fog in the valley. Our talk is still on the relationships with these adult children of ours. With my incessant questions, I am getting to know yours better than you are getting to know mine. I had never gotten to know you and your family nearly this well. This is good.

I now know something of all of your children. You told me about the struggles of your son and your passion to want to help him, of the strained relationship with your daughter since her marriage and the move to Chicago, and finally of parenting your young "princess" who isn't setting any land speed records at achieving her own personal maturity.

Your concern is obvious—as is how intentional you have been at parenting. Nurture is clearly a part of your soul. You have been attentive. You haven't missed much. You know your children, their friends, and the world in which they grew up. It's not the one we knew, of course. Not even close.

Before the others come out to join us, let's step back for a moment to take in that broader view.

SIR KEN ROBINSON, an authority on education and creativity, was speaking at a conference and asked all in the audience who were older than twenty-five years old to raise their hands. A large percentage did so. Then he asked of the same group how many were wearing watches. The same number of hands went up.

He said the result would be decidedly different with a younger audience. Young adults have a different mind-set on so many things—like carting around a "single-function device," as his daughter called it. (To which he protested, "No, no, it tells the date as well!")[1]

Though watches are beginning to make a comeback with young adults as a matter of style, they remain a symbol of our different worlds. In countless ways, theirs is a different mind-set shaped by living in a different world.[2]

THEIR WORLD

These days we run the danger of stereotyping generations, each with their letter label—X, Y, and even Z—as if every member of that generation would fit in lockstep with its description.

They don't, of course. Each member of every generation is unique. Yet there are patterns, and there is value in understanding the patterns of these generations. Members of these different eras are not identical to one another, but they have much in common; their lives are shaped by shared influences and parallel experiences.

Some who write of recent history get quite precise about how to define each of these generations, but for our purposes we'll round it off and include in Generation X those born between 1965 and 1980 and in Generation Y those born between 1981 and 1995. Before that was the Greatest Generation, comprised of those born between 1900 and 1924, the Traditionalists, born between 1925 and 1945, and the Baby Boomers, born between 1946 and 1964.

The vast majority of our adult children are considered to be from Generation X or Y. Most of us parents are Baby Boomers, though some of the oldest from Generation X now have adult children.

Why is looking at this important? Because these young whippersnappers have many

different attitudes,

different life perspectives,

different objectives,

different priorities,

different lifestyles . . . from the rest of us.

13

Different, and in some ways better—more balanced, relational, and family oriented. Young adults today bring some wonderful qualities. They not only are more available for relationship but also are the kind of people with whom we can enjoy being in relationship.

Let's take this time to get to know our young adults better. I can't love someone I don't know. If I want to love my adult son or daughter meaningfully, then I have to get to know him or her and his or her attitudes, views, and life perspectives.

Naturally, the first and best way to do this is through our personal relationships with our adult children. There is but one of each of them—they are each unique, and they are the best teachers of who they are. "But I already know my own kids," we want to say. Well, yes and no. There is indeed so much we do know from those two decades of rearing them, but they are at a new place now—with new aspirations, new challenges, new anxieties, and new hopes.

We do know them, but do we know them now? Have they made transitions with which we need to catch up?

Take the time. Sit down. No distractions. Catch up. Not only do you get to know them better—and they get to know you—but also, in the course of this intimate conversation, an already rich relationship is enhanced and deepened.

There is no substitute for getting to know our daughters and sons face-to-face, up close and personal. Yet I also find it useful to get to know them as a generation. It's like remaining focused on the same subject but switching to a wide-angle lens. Understanding their generations can lead to a deeper respect and connection. Not understanding can lead to unnecessary consternation.

When I read descriptions of generations X and Y, I find it remarkable how accurate this data is, as I match it up with the young adults I know. And having a son and a daughter of each generation, I know them and their friends well. Let's look for a moment at the defining characteristics of our adult sons and daughters as a part of Gen X and Gen Y. Generally, what these two generations have in common are the following:

They are more focused on family and relationships than on work.

They see themselves working in multiple places and careers over their lives.

They are tech savvy.

They are comfortable with change.

There is much in common between these generations, but there are also differences.

GENERATION X

Those of Generation X are often portrayed as being more negative than they likely deserve to be. This is understandable. There is a sense of pushing against what they have seen in their parents' attitudes and lifestyles. Anytime one disagrees or rebels, it may not be pretty. Yet, however awkwardly they have rebelled, the attitudes and priorities toward which they were trying to move were usually positive.

Gen Xers grew up seeing their parents work awfully hard for the family but felt their parents neglected the family in the process. We parents were taught to keep our noses to the grindstone, but our children wish we had not been so devoted to what they saw as our imbalanced view of responsibility.[3] I think of these lyrics from Reba McEntire's song "The Greatest Man I Never Knew": "I never really knew him, and now it seems so sad. Everything he gave to us took all he had."[4]

Their perception of this imbalance had a powerful effect. They entered their adulthood determined to bring balance to their lives. Family and friendships are important to them. In pushing away from their parents' dedication to work, GenXers emphasized relationships, not work. It has been said about Generation Xers, "They don't live to work; they work to live."[5]

Many feel a second effect of Gen Xers' perception that they were neglected as children is an overdependence on their parents in young adulthood. Those who study generational differences point to the increased tendency by members of Gen X to rely on their parents for money, time helping them, and assistance with child care. This is the first generation to have delayed taking full adult responsibility until about age thirty.[6]

Then there is another dynamic at play that appears to be in contradiction to this delayed responsibility. In fact, it seems to stand beside it as an interesting irony. During the childhoods of those in Generation X, many mothers began entering the workforce, making this the first generation of latchkey children. Many feel this led to an increased attitude of independence and self-sufficiency—an attitude, as we said, not always matched by an assumption of responsibility.[7]

They also saw their dedicated, hardworking parents extend great loyalty to their employers and after many years of service get no loyalty in return. This was a tragic mistake, in their eyes, which they will never duplicate. In sharp contrast to their parents, they see much less correlation between hard work and success.

Not only will they never commit to one employer, but also having multiple careers is a definite possibility for most of them. Change is a part of their temperament across the board, and that will most certainly include their professional lives.

GENERATION Y—THE MILLENNIALS

Generation Y, also known as the Millennial Generation, is large in number. Some have called them the "Echo Boomers," reflecting the similar population size to Baby Boomers. They will be the bulk of the U.S. population by 2020. We will give Gen Y even more attention, since most reading this are likely new to being parents of young adults—hence, the parents of Gen Y.

Members of this generation are more optimistic, confident, and happy with their lives.[8] They believe in themselves and are primed to achieve. They believe they will be successful in attaining whatever they wish to accomplish.

They are sometimes referred to as the Millennial Generation since Gen Y may imply they are simply an extension of Gen X, which they clearly are not. With this generation, it is truly a new day.

Though those in Gen Y are similar in age to those in Gen X, they grew up in a different world from that of Gen X. They had more parental involvement and supervision as the parenting pendulum swung from the latchkey era. There was more emphasis on team sports and play dates than in any preceding generation. It is no surprise then that, as adults, they are community and team oriented.[9]

They are more eager than Gen Xers to go to work, but they want to participate in decisions and are not shy about asking questions or giving their input, requested or not. They want mentors whom they respect and from whom they can learn. They want to be challenged.[10] They seek feedback and, hopefully, affirmation. Some boomer managers consider their Gen Y employees to be high performance and high maintenance.[11] Much of this has changed recently, of course. Some of their motivation and lofty professional expectations have slammed into the wall of a struggling economy in which they now feel fortunate to get any job.

Like the previous generation, they want independence and balance to their lives. They are devoted to their friends and want to have plenty of time with their families.[12]

Their interest in being well educated is notably high. Many are working and completing their education at the same time. An interest in religion is remarkably low. The percentage with a religious affiliation is significantly lower than in previous generations.[13]

They are delaying rites of passage into adulthood. They are waiting until later to get married. They are living with their parents longer, even before the economic recession made it necessary for many of them.

GEN Y'S CHILDHOOD:
"EVERYBODY GETS A TROPHY"

In recent decades, concern grew among parents and teachers over our children's self-esteem. It became a focus of apprehension as self-esteem came to be seen as fragile and in need of intentional care.

So, across our society, we sought to address the problem. Children were taught to affirm themselves with "I am great." There was an increased timidity to discipline. Nothing was to be done that could damage their potentially fragile self-esteem. Everything was to affirm.[14] A shopping trip through a Babies "R" Us will expose one to such affirming messages as "Chick Magnet," "Supermodel," "Princess," and "I'm the Boss" on bibs and onesies.[15]

Guess what? In those same decades in which we were so attentive to bolster our children's sense of how wonderful they were, research shows that what increased was not their self-esteem but their narcissism.[16] This sense of personal importance is seen in the "look at me" attitude behind much of Twitter, blogs, and Facebook—obsessing over the details of what one is doing much of the day.

The problem with this everybody-gets-a-trophy philosophy is that everybody gets a trophy—whether they worked for it or not. The message went out that you win by showing up. Effort, commitment, dedication, and self-discipline may be desirable but are optional. One comic strip showed a child standing in his soccer uniform in the foyer of his home. He was clearly just back from a match, and beside him was his trophy, almost as tall as he was. Speaking to a family member who had not attended the game, he said, "And we almost won!"

Yes, there is a direct correlation between our increased concern about our children's self-esteem and their increased narcissism. As parents, we bring rational thought back into this and realize that:

We love our children for who they are.

We affirm and encourage them for the potential we see in them, but for heaven's sake, we reserve our praise until something is shown to be praiseworthy.

Self-esteem can't be given to our children. We were well intentioned in our efforts to praise and affirm, but we may have neglected building character. Self-esteem can't be built. Self-esteem is a result of a life of character and integrity. If parents help their children truly build lives of character, children will have all the self-esteem they can handle.

Even though it looks as if we facilitated in them a sense of entitlement, we gave them something else as well. Before we get too negative with the entitlement that resulted, let's be aware that the Millennials also have remarkable optimism, confidence, and positive attitudes. If their inflation has them thinking they can leap tall buildings with a single bound, their optimism may encourage them to clear a short one. It is the idea of the self-fulfilling prophecy at work, and they will be the beneficiaries of it.

It is my opinion that the optimism and positive spirit these young adults display are less connected with the "you are wonderful" message parents gave them than with the fact that parents were involved, interacting, and being engaged, whatever the message. They were loved. Their parents cared. It was hands-on parenting. Gen Xers were right that the boomers had become too focused on career and wisely reminded us of the need for balance. Parents became hands-on, and the new confidence of this Generation Y is one of the results.

SHAPED BY TECHNOLOGY

Generation Y is the most plugged-in generation. They have never known a day without electronic contact. It has been said that Gen Xers are comfortable with technology. For those in Generation Y, it's much more than comfort. They are in constant, instant communication and are extremely peer oriented. They stay in touch. Texting is almost like talking. It's second nature.

Here is one of the pluses for us parents about all this communicating: across the board, Gen Yers stay in touch with their parents more than any other generation. In a Pew Research Center survey, three in four of those in Gen Y reported that they see their parents at least once a week, and more than 80 percent said they talked with their parents in the past day.[17] They may be consistently wired, but they are using their electronics to contact us. (Of course, before we get too misty-eyed about this, they also acknowledge that these conversations often have to do with money—that is, receiving it.)

But money and the technological ease of staying in touch aside, those in Generation Y consistently say they feel close to their parents. They value the relationship with their parents unlike in any previous generation.[18]

Did I give you too much information about these generations? That's a lot to take in. So let's summarize. The characteristics that distinguish Generation X from the previous baby boomers are:

They are highly independent.

They are tech savvy.

They are focused on family and relationships.

They are determined not to let work dominate their lives.

They are comfortable with change.

Generation Y has continued to embody most of the above—but with several new features:

They like to achieve.

They are optimistic and positive.

They work as a team.

They crave attention.

They believe in themselves.

They always will love things electronic that allow them to communicate.

OUR TAKE-AWAY

What can we learn from all of this? I have already spoken to some of the concerns to which this data points, such as the delayed sense of responsibility and the potential for narcissism. But frankly, there is much about which we can and should feel positive.

Our adult children embrace relationships like no other generation before them. As they are intentional about this, their marriages may be more intimately connected, their families closer, and their friendships more valued. Building on that passion for relationships is how they like to work as a team and love to stay connected, via any electronic means possible. This points to a future in which community—a close, caring community—may well be reclaimed while it is also redefined.

Our relationship with them is a part of this. They value us. I know, I know. There are exceptions. And there are times they don't make our value to them really obvious. And, of course, there are times it seems as if it is all about what we can do for them. But they value us. This is a new time in their lives. Much of the authoritarian structure that defined our relationship is fading, as are old resentments. The result is that they often rediscover the love and closeness they feel for their parents.[19]

Young adults really do feel closer to us. That is both what the data clearly shows and what my personal experience and observations continue to confirm. Some have accused us of being overly invested in their lives, and there is truth to that. But we were involved. We cared about them, and they knew it. We connected with them. Now they want to remain connected with us.

My wife, Karen, and I are blessed to have a wonderful group of friends. Virtually all have young adult children. As we are in and out of one another's homes, I see parents and their children together. I see them hanging out, laughing, and clearly enjoying one another. I hear of the questions their daughters bring to them. I hear of the decisions their sons want to talk out with them. Our sons and daughters value us. And we value them. The potential is there for real and lasting relationships.

GENERATIONAL DIFFERENCES

I'm not sure the phrase "generational differences" quite gets it. The differences in the worlds of our generations are vast. It is remarkable how quickly and how radically the world changes. Our sons and daughters were born in a different time, with different influences and different life experiences from us—thus, they are going to engage life differently. It's a given.

There is much we have to learn from them, and it's not just about operating cell phones and computers. Their different perspective brings ideas and insights we could never have imagined. There is also much they have to learn from us, but they will still come at life differently. My parents went through the Great Depression and World War II. Their perspectives were clearly shaped from these life experiences. It was a different world and a different worldview from mine. I could—and did—learn from theirs. But I was not of theirs.

Our adult children can—and hopefully will—learn from our worldview. But ours is not theirs either. There are pluses to each worldview. But to the point: they come at much of life differently. We must respect that there are, and will be, differences. Don't keep pushing what they don't seem to get. If it is important, life will teach them. It's as I have said to countless parents of teenagers: "I so hope they will learn that lesson from you. Because if they don't, life will teach it to them later on. And you teach it with love. Life won't."

3

Resetting the Sails

*Breakfast always tastes better in the mountains. While half
of our crew cleans away the table and begins with the
dishes, those of us who did the cooking remain at the table.
You and I were among the chefs who now lean back in our
chairs as the conversation takes whatever turn it chooses.
Sports, world affairs, news updates, aging parents—
absolutely no politics—and children. We all have grown
children. We all have our stories about the joys and trials
of being the parents of adults.*

*Todd puts some strawberry preserves on his last scrap of
toast as he laughs about how confusing it all is these days.
"Adult children," he says. "What in the world does that
mean? 'Adult children.' Isn't that one of those oxymorons?
Which are they, adults or children? And what does that*

27

make them when they were kids, 'children children'? No
wonder we don't know how to relate to them. We don't
even have a name for them that makes any sense."

We settle back in our chairs. Todd is on a roll. "Well,
back in my day it was all pretty straightforward. None of
this ambiguity. You grew up, went to college, graduated in
exactly four years, got a job that same week, married your
college sweetheart, had your two kids, and you were off to
the races—just like God intended.

"But all of that has changed. You think you have them
about to be educated, soon to be employed, and they are
off to the Rockies for a year to find themselves or get an
apartment somewhere in Europe to experience the world.
It's all so different."

TODD IS RIGHT. So much is different now. When adulthood actually begins is even ambiguous these days. As he said, it used to be when we finished our education and got jobs. We were self-sustaining and independent, hence *adults*. The traditional milestones for adulthood—leaving home, becoming financially independent, marrying, and having a child—just don't fit anymore.[1] In 1960, 70 percent of thirty-year-olds had achieved these milestones. By 2000, it was fewer than 40 percent.[2] To today's young adults, such milestones likely appear outdated, quaint, and even amusing.

The criteria for adulthood today are not events or milestones such as graduation or marriage, but criteria that are gradual, evolving. They include:

Accepting responsibility for yourself;

making independent decisions;

becoming financially independent.[3]

Arriving at adulthood is not so simple anymore. Traditional societal standards are not going to define the lifestyles of these young adults. With a finger on the pulse of what has integrity for them, what fits them, they are in charge of their own lives, thank you very much. They will arrive at these milestones for adulthood in whatever order they choose and in a time frame that fits them.

Now, fellow parents, having just written the above paragraphs, I am aware of how rebellious and "so stick it in your ear" their attitude could appear. Yet across the board, that is not the way it feels. They don't seem angry to me. Of course, there are exceptions. But today's young adults seem positive, optimistic—even a bit idealistic—and enthusiastic to carve out lives that are authentic and have integrity for them.

And these days there is one other way the old norms don't fit. In our new economy they struggle to get jobs. Or they get jobs and then are laid off; they move out of our homes into their own places and then, out of financial necessity, they move back in. The old standards don't apply anymore.

At this new place, as parents of adult children, we are looking for the balance—the balance between nurturing our adult sons and daughters while encouraging their independence and maturity.

We are looking for the balance:

29

How are we supportive, yet not intrusive?

How are we available, yet not pushy?

How are we caring, yet not enabling dependency?

As our daughters and sons move into young adulthood, our understanding of what it means to be loving parents continues to change. It's a transition toward their independence that has been in process all of their lives—a movement toward individuation, as it is called.

Remember our first two touchstones—the two that are exclusively about them.

To help them move forward into this new chapter of their lives.

To help them achieve their full maturity as adults.

Let's be guided by them as we make this crucial transition.

When it comes to parenting adult children, in one way, it's a lot like parenting them when they were children—there is no one size fits all. It's unique to each child. Each adult child is different, and each parent's relationship with each child has a different chemistry. There is no set model.

We are aware that this move toward independence and maturity is a process—as is our relationship with them. There is nothing abrupt about the shifts from relating with them as children to adolescents to adults. I mentioned earlier the parting ceremony that many colleges have for the parents of incoming freshmen on the day they arrive. I understand the intent of this as a symbolic reminder that we are to respect the independence of our sons and daughters who are now college students and young adults. This is in marked contrast to how we have been encouraged to be closely involved in every grade level from preschool through secondary school.

Change can happen abruptly. Transition evolves. Relationships are about transition. College freshmen don't need hovering parents. Some may want to be turned loose and left alone. Others may need continued support, guidance, and nurture. Then there are those who may want regularly to enjoy sharing the new experiences college brings with their parents, who remain important to them. We look for the healthy balance in the relationship with each child.[4]

It's a lot like marriage. There is no one right way to do it. Every marriage is made up of two unique individuals, so it's a given that their relationship will also be unique. Yet there are solid, healthy, connecting principles to being married that apply to us all.

It's the same with parenting adult children. As soon as I come up with anything resembling a model—a set of principles to define how to go about doing this parenting—I can think of a thousand exceptions and can "yes, but" it to death. Not only is each child unique, but also there are all the unique circumstances and crises that come up in their lives. So, again, there are never one-size-fits-all solutions, but there are principles to guide us. Let's begin with those.

CARING <u>FOR</u> THEM WITHOUT TAKING CARE <u>OF</u> THEM

How we engage with this new relationship involves the distinction between *caring* and *taking care of*. *Caring*, as I am using the term, means doing for our adult children what they can't do for themselves. This is healthy and loving.

Taking care of—and this is not healthy—is doing for your adult children what they can do for themselves or what they can now develop the capacity to do for themselves. *Taking care of* an adult son or daughter encourages dependency, and the relationship often becomes codependent. It's not a pretty sight. I always think of Matthew McConaughey's character in the movie *Failure to Launch* shoveling away those pancakes as his mother hovers over him, meeting her adult son's every need.

Many young adults, who don't naturally develop maturity and responsibility, continue to cling to their parents. Some are simply late bloomers and genuinely haven't reached that level of maturity. Others are milking the system for all they can get out of it, appearing needier than they really are. Still others are living out the philosophy we discussed in the preceding chapter of waiting until about thirty to claim their full adulthood. As parents, we have to discern if we are doing for them what they can't yet do for themselves or if we are allowing an unhealthy dependency that should end.

In some cases parents may encourage ongoing dependency.

What? What was that? Why would a parent *choose* to perpetuate an old relationship for which time has passed? Some parents may have an investment or a personal motivation in not changing the relationship because subconsciously they are getting some-thing out of it. Again, this usually is happening subconsciously. This is not an accusation. These are fine parents who would do nothing intentionally to harm their children or their development, but they are contributing to their son's or daughter's ongoing dependence by allowing it or even encouraging it.

It may be a version of the overused term *codependency*. In its broader use, the term simply means that the dependency goes both ways. It is mutual. These parents have a stake in the caretak-ing relationship remaining largely as it has been. They have "a dog in the hunt," as we say in the South.

Parents who continue to take care of their adult sons or daughters often are doing it out of their own need to be needed, even at the expense of their adult children's maturity. In the lan-guage of the recovery movement, they become enablers of their child's ongoing dependency. Either parent may experience a resistance to make the transition, out of the fear of the loss of the relationship that was or the fear of the emptiness in their own lives now that they aren't primarily parents.

This new empty-nest chapter may feel more associated with anxiety than opportunity. These parents know and enjoy the meaning and fulfillment that came from parenting, but they aren't so sure where they will find it in this new world. This is true for the mom who has so much self-identity connected with actively parenting. Then, to be fair to both genders, there is the father of a "daddy's girl" who wouldn't do anything that might risk the loss of the precious relationship with his daughter.

Other parents may find that what they are getting out of it is related to an overly zealous desire to be liked by their children. They know parenting isn't a popularity contest, but they can't stand for their adult children to be upset with them. Some children take advantage of this and use it as a form of intimidation. Just ask any teacher you know, of any grade level, how many parents they have seen over the years who are afraid of their own children.

Then there are parents with deeply protective personalities who are now interfering with a healthy transition process. It may be related to subconscious echoes from their young adulthoods when they were anxious about assuming adult responsibilities of their own. At any point in children's lives, parents subconsciously revisit their own lives at that age—along with any unresolved issues. These anxieties can get projected onto their children, and then the parents may feel the need to protect the children from dangers they experienced when they were young adults.

In other families, the parents may be intrusive out of the illusion of caring for their children, but in reality they are simply controlling because they need to be in control. Their adult children may be mature and responsible, but Mom or Dad still wants to run parts of their lives. This does not enable dependency—it creates resentment. Mom may come into town for a visit with her daughter and, while the daughter is at work, rearrange the pictures or furniture in the house "just so it looks a little nicer." You can count on a chill in the air as they have dinner together that evening.

We must make the transition. I think of the quotation I once came across, "People only accept change in necessity and see necessity only in crisis." We must see the necessity—remembering our touchstones—begin the transition, and not wait for the relational crisis that eventually would come.

Caring is a good thing. *Taking care of* is not. But where is the line? Where does my caring leave off and my adult child pick up? Where does my responsibility end and his or hers begin? Again, *caring* for our adult children is doing for them what they can't do for themselves. It is good, healthy, and loving. *To take care of* them is to do for them what they can, and should, do for themselves. *To take care of* them is also to do for them what they can't do only because they have never been called on to develop that ability for which they have the potential.

As with much of life, it's usually a judgment call, and we'll come back to this. But please keep the distinction in mind, so we can be intentional about these decisions.

LET GO OF THE CONTROLS

Power and control—I don't want them. I have plenty to say grace over running my own life. I don't want control over adult children's lives. Which is fortunate because I don't *have* any control over their lives.

They will, and should, make the decisions for their lives. But even if I had power over their decisions, I hope I wouldn't use it, however tempted. I want them to feel their full adult, personal authority.

I think of a comment Karen's mom once made to her, referring to how gracious, yet how strong she always had been. She said to Karen, "You always listened to what I said, and then you did what you had to do."

I don't want them to have *authority issues*. Whenever someone has an authority issue, usually that person's issue focuses on the relationship with a professor or a boss or any authoritative figure whom the young adult feels is intimidating. Yet, though the focus is on the relationship, the real authority issue is about the young adult not having claimed his or her personal authority—thus continuing to project it onto someone else.

Having learned from those whose judgment they respect, young adults increasingly need to develop their personal authority and to listen to the wisdom of its voice. I want them to hear and value and act out of their personal depth.

The only way they can achieve the full stature of their personal authority is if we parents remain lovingly supportive while we are clear they are in charge of their lives, their directions, and their decisions. Our prayer is that they claim that authority for themselves and that they make those decisions wisely.

It seems to happen most often in the springtime. A middle-aged couple bring their eighteen-year-old daughter to my office for counseling. I ask them what brought them to counseling. Their daughter—let's call her Julie—sits with arms crossed, silently glaring at her parents on the sofa. Her father begins by describing their concern about the young man she is dating. Mom jumps into the conversation with an animated and irritated description of his rudeness, crudeness, and disrespect: "We have no idea what she sees in him or why she gives him the time of day! It just isn't the way she was reared."

After several minutes, when she can stand it no more, Julie unleashes her defense of Jimmy. Essentially, she says he is a diamond in the rough, but her parents can see none of the diamond in him.

Back and forth the conversation goes. I ask questions for clarity and information. At the end of the session, I ask Julie if she would be willing to meet with me by herself. Unfailingly, she says yes.

When we meet the following week, she picks up where she left off with an impassioned statement in defense of her rough diamond. She talks and talks until she begins to realize that I'm not her parents' representative. I simply want to get to know her and see how I can be helpful. Her tone then softens and her cadence slows. Before you know it, Julie begins to tell me the rest of the story. Yep, Jimmy can be a bit of a jerk at times. Fairly often, she says, he irritates the stew out of her too.

The next week I meet with her parents. I don't betray the confidentiality of the session with Julie. Among the many issues we discuss, I likely make one suggestion: "If you can say this with authenticity and integrity, tell Julie, 'We don't see what you see in Jimmy. But we know what we see in you, and that is a fine young woman who has our respect and trust. We believe in you. So, if you see Jimmy as someone worthy of dating, then go right ahead. We may not believe in him, but we believe in you.'"

Within three weeks, Julie has either broken up with Jimmy for how he treats her or has brought the relationship to a crisis in no longer tolerating his behavior.

What happened? Mom and Dad stepped back. They hushed, and Julie began hearing her own voice. They stepped back from assuming responsibility for her decisions, and she stepped forward to take responsibility for her life.

Humorist Lewis Grizzard said, "A man isn't a man until his father tells him so."[5] This is similar to the Old Testament idea of "the blessing." It is a rite of passage into adulthood. It affirms that adulthood. It can happen, of course, to both genders. It releases them to be the persons they are, to set their sails, to chart their course. It's something the Jewish faith does with a beautiful intentionality. When he gets there, tell him. When she arrives at her womanhood, tell her. It's far more than a compliment. It's a genuine, positive affirmation to them. It's our declaration of their independence. They are now adults making adult decisions, which we hope and pray are made wisely.

Give them *the blessing*. Tell them that you are not stepping away but that you are stepping *out of their way*; not that you are disconnecting, but you are reconnecting in a way that respects, affirms, and celebrates their adulthood.

In the movie *Secretariat*, on the night before this magnificent thoroughbred ran the last race of the Triple Crown, his owner said to him what her father had once spoken to her: "I've run my race. Now you run yours."

Power and control—that's the last thing we want over our children's lives. It holds them back, and, heck, it holds us back. We have worked hard for this empty nest. It's *our* declaration of *their* independence—it is good for us. But far more important, it's good for them.

The only way they can learn independence is if they know they are fully in charge and will either *enjoy* the consequences of wise choices or *suffer* the consequences of poor ones. I love the way a friend of mine put it recently: "Experience is a much better teacher than advice." We don't want them to learn the way we learned—hard knocks, sink or swim, trial and error—but, of course, they will.

FROM PARENT TO PEER

Psychiatrist Eric Berne, through his psychological theory of transactional analysis, gave us an understanding of three different ways we relate to life: as a Parent, as a Child, and as an Adult. Note that he capitalized each to distinguish these parts of ourselves from an actual parent or a child. He refers to these three as "ego states," but don't worry about that. We are interested in the simple clarity of recognizing these parts of ourselves with which we live and out of which we relate. Each of us has all three within us.[6]

If I relate out of my Parent, I am the authority; out of my Child, I defer; and from my Adult, I relate as a peer, an equal. Obviously, as parents to our young children, we relate out of the Parent part of ourselves, and they, the Child. As the years pass and they no longer are children, if it is to go well, a transition must take place. As my son and daughter mature into adulthood, we increasingly connect as fellow adults.

This is the goal: for it to be adult to adult. Not parent to child. Peer to peer. We move from parenthood to peer-ship, which is a relationship based on mutuality. I learn from them, and they from me. We enjoy each other. We respect each other as fellow adults. I may have far more years, but each of us has life experience, lessons learned, and sets of skills and abilities to offer the other.

Remember our third touchstone:

To establish a new, loving relationship with them—adult to adult.

Some parents make this adult-to-adult transition rather smoothly. They have anticipated this time and the transition it brings. They describe this change as being tough at times—"But they are still babes in the woods, and we have so much to teach them"—but they know this is the time they had anticipated. This is the moment to say good-bye to the perspective of parent to child and welcome the equally loving connection of adult to adult.

Other parents don't make the move from parent to peer as easily. This is not a new phenomenon. The mothers of both President Franklin Roosevelt and General Douglas MacArthur moved to live near their sons when they went to college.[7]

We can understand the struggle for many parents in making the transition. After decades of actively parenting, they feel as if they are dropping the ball, not being responsible. This is especially true for those parents from my generation, who have hovered over their children from T-ball to calculus. For other parents, it is frankly more self-serving. As I mentioned before, they get so much meaning, identity, and fulfillment out of being hands-on parents, they don't want to give it up. But it is time. It is time for their age, independence, and hopefully maturity to be recognized and shown the respect they deserve.

Adult-to-adult implies a friendship. One is a bit older with a few more miles of experience, but they are friends nonetheless. An indication of that friendship—and I hear this regularly from young adults—is to turn the tables and ask for their advice. "It makes me feel really good when they ask my opinion" is how a young woman said it recently. If they are coming over for a Fourth of July picnic, divide the load, and have them share in the preparation. Friendship always goes both ways.

National Public Radio has a weekly feature called Story Corps, in which people share their life stories. One Saturday morning I heard Nancy Wright telling the story of her relationship with her mother on this series. Their relationship had gone well until Nancy's teenage years when she became openly resistant to her mom's constant judgment and criticism.

This tension continued for years until they spent a particularly miserable weekend together. Nancy was then about thirty years old and had had enough. She told her mom that her criticism wasn't helpful and she couldn't deal with it any longer. Her mother said, "But that's what mothers do." Nancy responded that she "didn't need a mother anymore. I needed a friend."

Her mother was angry, and since stubbornness is "kind of a family trait," Nancy didn't expect to hear from her. She didn't—for about two weeks. Then, in Nancy's words, "I picked up the phone one day and a kind of small voice said on the other side, 'Hi, this is your friend.' "[8]

RESPECT THEIR NEED FOR OUR BOUNDARIES

It has been said, "The only difference between a river and a swamp is the river has boundaries." I have consciously attempted to put in place healthy, self-imposed boundaries that allow for our adult children's growth toward maturity and for the flow of our relationship. These are the boundaries that restrain me—boundaries keeping me from my intrusiveness—boundaries that rein me in from trying to run their lives. I think, *Keep it to yourself, Ron.* If I don't honor that boundary, what I do is pushy, disrespectful, and counterproductive. Our adult children personally—and our relationship together—will suffer the consequences.

They are just like we were way back then: excited about the freedom, a little anxious, and with much to learn. As parents, our hearts are in the right place. But some of us parents are eager—some, desperate—to spoon-feed these lessons to our adult children so they don't have to learn these lessons the way we did, through trial and error. It usually doesn't work. With adult children, the more intrusive we are—no matter how caring our motives—the more they will resist, and rightly so. They have to remind us they are no longer children. The main result of being pushy parents is damaging the relationship and leaving both parties isolated.

Whenever we are intrusive, what they hear is not the lesson we are trying to share but the message that we don't really respect that they are now grown.

I know there are exceptions such as struggles with health concerns, maturity gaps, substance abuse issues, situations of spousal abuse, or financial crises that may call for intervention. Of course, we're not about to sit back when faced with these.

Intervention in these circumstances is not intrusion—it's loving. This is not disrespecting their adulthood—I would do the same for a friend and expect that friend to do the same for me. I'm not about to let something tragic happen to my adult child because I might seem pushy.

We will come back to the unique circumstances and crises in our children's lives in a later chapter. Here our focus is on the mainstream of our relationships with our adult children, and that river must have appropriate boundaries to avoid intrusion. We set and maintain those boundaries. We love them and will not intrude inappropriately into their lives.

ALWAYS AVAILABLE

In the midst of all the talk of boundaries, emerging adulthood, and respect for their independence, let's not forget that we are still absolutely there for them and always will be. I know you have said to each of your adult children some form of, "Please know we are always here for you. Never hesitate to call."

But when they call, for what will they likely be calling? When they need us, for what will they need us?

It is often money and rarely advice.

Let's face it, for the most part, the days of teaching our children are *so over*. That cow is out of the barn. Yet there may well be times when we do receive a call for guidance. Remember the adage: "When the student is ready, the teacher appears." To tweak it slightly: when adult students have a question and know Mom and Dad are not going to try to ram ideas down their throats, they may call us.

Especially regarding advice, we let them know we are available for ideas, guidance, and support. We will be open, candid, and honest. We will not be pushy or controlling. And then we wait for the time when the student is ready.

But from here on our influence won't be pontificating, which was never influential anyway. Our effect may be as important—just different. They will face an important decision or a difficult dilemma and will need to talk it out. They will be hit with a real disappointment or even heartache and will need to be heard. We will be there for them as a quiet sounding board (though that "quiet" part is not necessarily our long suit). We will not push ourselves or our ideas on them. We are there for one of the critical functions of any loving relationship—to listen.

Because we have been there, we know that they need to talk and be heard. It can be transforming. We have had those crucial times when "I really felt heard" and felt it as grace. Those are moments of profound intimacy.

43

Stephen Covey worded the truth well when he wrote, "Most people do not listen with the intent to understand; they listen with the intent to reply. They're either speaking or preparing to speak."[9] When we listen to those we love, we listen to understand, to support, and to be drawn more closely.

For our sons and daughters, this is their first time at adulthood. There will be so much that is new that they may need to talk through it as they come to understand who they are in this new place. Mostly, this will require our patience, our support, and our silence. Listen. They will need some guidance, some pearls of wisdom, but first they need our quiet listening as we take in their every word.

They will tell you what they need, if anything, beyond that. Having listened to my children in times past, I've heard myself ask, "Would you like some feedback?" "No, I'm good," I may hear. And they are.

There is another way we are available to these young adults of ours. That is simply to enjoy the relationship. Our days of parental heavy lifting are over. So much responsibility is gone from the relationship. It's time to enjoy them. Have the time for them. Initiate the time together. Become the best of friends. Talk about the latest book you've read. Play a round of golf. Ask how the job is going. Take each of them to dinner. Connect with them. Show them how much they mean to you.

I remember learning that the way to a man's heart truly was through his stomach when our son, Patrick, was a young man and still single. I was never turned down when I invited him to meet me for dinner. And I got the pleasure of my son's company. No one else was invited. Just the two of us. I highly recommend it.

MODEL WHAT WE WANT THEM TO LEARN

As I said, the days of teaching our children are over. Or are they?

Remember that great quotation from Mahatma Gandhi, "Be the change you want to see in the world." From here on with our young adults, unless there is an extreme need, the single best way we can have input is to model it. To tweak Gandhi's words: be the change you want to see in the lives of the next generation.

As adults—much like when they were children—they learn more from what they see than from what they hear. Telling them may make us feel better. It may feel like we've really done something, though we likely haven't done much. Showing them communicates far better. As it was once said, "Preach the gospel at all times and when necessary use words."

Countless times I have heard a middle-aged parent say, "I just don't know what to do about my daughter. She is just like me in that she always . . ." as she goes on to describe one of their less-than-desirable mutual traits. "Do you really want to help her with that?" I'll ask. "Of course I do," the parent replies. "I know too well what a burden it is. I would just do anything if I could help her."

"There is really only one way you can help," I say. "But it can be very useful to her. *Show her how.* Make the change in you that you want to see in her. Model it. Show her that it can be done, and show her how to do it."

Model it. Are you one of those parents who privately wishes you could have been a bigger influence on your children as they were growing up? Maybe you were too busy or didn't know how to go about it. Maybe you had some maturing to do and were still rather self-absorbed. Many parents tell me they just weren't in the game and feel badly about it. If that applies to you, first, remember that none of us can be great at every phase of parenting. This may be your time.

If you weren't so great at it before, it's not too late. Of course, it is far too late to lecture, but that method never worked so well at any phase.

What works is to model it. Show them. Be it for them. Be what you want them to see. Live what you want them to learn.

There is one other way modeling can be helpful. For years young adults have told me they just don't see much to look forward to when they look at the lives of those over thirty—"present company excepted," they hasten to add. Life, for them, seems to be over at adulthood. In the last chapter, titled "Empty Nest," I will encourage you to make the most of this time of your life for your sake. Here is an additional reason: for their sake. Model what it is like to be a middle-aged or older adult and thoroughly enjoy your life. Show them that adulthood may actually be something to which they can look forward. Have fun. Engage in what fulfills you. Show them.

4

Respecting Their Need for Respect

There is a breeze in the mountain air as we head out on
our traditional late morning hike. We take the easier route
up the mountainside, though we well remember how the
climb gets pretty steep as we near the summit. But it's
always worth it—the scenery, the vistas, the company, and
the picnic together at the very top.

Getting up the mountain isn't quite the same as it once
was. We've been coming here for years. We were all getting
sitters for our preschoolers when we began these weekends
away. We laugh and understand when, about halfway up,
you said, "Wasn't this mountain shorter back in the old
days? I promise you this section wasn't nearly as steep
either. And did we always sweat this much?"

Time has moved on. Much has changed. The mountain hasn't, but we have. This climb, really a vigorous hike that once took an hour and a half tops, now takes two minimum.

Much has changed. Some changes we regret. Some we celebrate. All of them we need to acknowledge—and respect. The mountain takes more effort. Not bad, not good, just different.

There. Made it. We spread out the tablecloth on the granite outcropping at the mountain's peak. The seating is not comfortable, but the scenery, just as beautiful as we remember. It's always worth the climb. We'll take pictures of one another but never of the view. We learned long ago that no photo does it justice. Just can't capture it.

We dine on our traditional chicken salad sandwiches. It's Nancy's treat every year. Our unplanned conversational theme of the weekend continues, though it has taken a softer tone. Maybe that's what two hours of hiking will do. As we reflect together, the pauses are longer. We all seem more thoughtful as we wonder just what it is they need—these young adults of ours—what is it they need the most from us. Much has changed. They have changed. Their needs have changed.

We all have our stories about the times we have really messed up. Times we have marched boldly into the lives of these young adults just like we, long ago, marched into their rooms with their fifth-grade teacher's note in hand.

Elizabeth shakes her head as she remembers. "I just can't believe it. It was just a few months ago. I was standing there fussing at Ashley, telling her in precise detail exactly how she should run her life. I promise you, I was even pointing at her with this very index finger when it dawned on me . . .

"What am I doing? Holy cow, what in the world am I doing? I'll tell you what I'm doing. I'm lecturing in the most insulting, condescending way to a bright, insightful thirty-year-old wife, mother, and assistant district attorney. What was I doing? I was making an idiot of myself."

We laugh. And we remember. We have all been there. Every one of us. It's hard to break old habits. We've all had times we regress into the parents of old. That was then, and this is now, we try to remind ourselves.

MUCH HAS CHANGED. That was then, and this is now. The issue is: *What do they need at this new point of their lives?*

More than anything else, they need respect. Remember our goal, our touchstone in parenting young adults.

To help them achieve their full maturity as adults.

It's not about us. It's not about what we feel the need to teach them or want to get off our chest. It's about them and how we can help them thrive and grow and mature. In order to achieve this, what they need now is respect.

And remember our third goal:

49

To establish a new, loving relationship with them—adult to adult.

A cornerstone to loving relationships with grown daughters and sons is the attitude of respect that one adult has for another.

GIVING ADVICE

It has been my experience that the moment at which respect or disrespect is most clearly seen is when we are faced with the issue of giving advice to our young adult children. Few moments will convey respect—or the lack of it—like giving them direction on living their lives. Their intuitive radar will pick up on any signals that hint at the condescension of a parent talking *down* to a child. So, how do we do it? *How do we, as parents of adults, give advice?*

Let me begin (by stating boldly), "It depends." It depends on the context, the topic, the personalities, and many other variables; but most important, it depends on the relationship we have with them. Give advice respecting the unique relationship with that son or daughter.

When I listen to young adults talk about getting advice from their parents, their responses to that advice are all over the map. Some young adults will flat-out say they don't want *any* advice from their parents. None. "Absolutely not. I don't want it," they tell me.

Others count on it. "My mom knows me like nobody else, and she has all those years of experience. I want her ideas." From another: "I know nothing about investments. I count on my dad for that kind of thing." These young adults want parents to shoot straight. They want to know what their parents think. "Cool your jets" and "You're overreacting" are the kinds of responses one young woman told me she counts on from her mom. This woman and her mom are close, and this kind of directness is true to the nature of their relationship. This is the same young woman who told me, "Oh, I talk with my mom about five times a day." It's not dependency. It's not unhealthy. It's close. They are good friends. Not surprising, this is most often true between mothers and daughters.

All of these relationships may be loving, but some are closer than others, some more direct than others, and some more personal than others. Each wants respect but in different ways. How do your adult children want it? ASK THEM. Ask them how they feel about your giving advice, and you soon will be in the middle of a most interesting conversation. Expect it to be different for each of them. But there is one word of guidance I can give you that is common to all, no matter the chemistry: give advice with the respect you would give to any other adult, for that is who our daughters and sons have now become. To honor that respect opens the door to a healthy adult-to-adult relationship. Not to honor it is to hear the click of a door closing.

We know this issue of respect for our adult children gets complex. What they want is from one extreme to the other. You likely have a pretty good idea about each of your sons and daughters. You know their personalities, and you know the tone of your relationship with them. As a young woman described it, her parents' giving advice is "in keeping with the whole relationship."

Yet across the board, no one wants to be told what to do. No matter how close the relationship, avoid anything resembling *control.* One young man knew he had reached adulthood in his father's eyes when he heard, "What do you think you are going to do?" instead of being told what to do regarding an upcoming decision. It is probably significant that he remembers it word for word. He was touched by the respect.

Several times I have heard from appreciative young adults, always with a warm smile, that their parents' guidance came in the form of recalling their own experiences back when they were young. "Well, when I had to make that decision"—it sounded a lot like a conversation and very little like a lecture.

When you give advice, make it clear to your adult children that you are offering opinions for their consideration. You don't want to be intrusive, and you are not insulting their intelligence or maturity. I like the way author Ruth Nemzoff puts it: "Remind your children they don't have to take your advice and that your advice is only one piece of data in many they will gather."[1]

SOLICITED ADVICE

Situations that call for sharing our wisdom spring from two contexts: times when our counsel is sought and times when it is not (though we deeply feel the need to offer it). Let's begin with the easier one: when they come to us and directly ask for our guidance on a matter of importance to them.

Young adults tell me they periodically will seek their parents' advice: "College certainly didn't teach me everything. I call them about insurance or 401(k)s and say, 'Mom, Dad, what do I do?'" We love those moments when we can be helpful. It's still an adult-to-adult conversation, but we are helping. (We hope they love it, too, since next week we'll be calling them asking for help with downloading photos onto our computer.)

Other times they may come to us with a bigger issue—perhaps a decision about a job offer in a different city. We then are presented with such a temptation to pontificate. And it is totally justified—after all, *they asked us.* If you can—and this is tough to keep in focus—recall the touchstone: *to help them achieve their full maturity as adults.* Do everything you can do to remember to begin, "Sure I've got some ideas, but first what do you think?" Here you can kill the proverbial two birds with one toss of the stone. You encourage them to think it through for themselves, and you show your confidence in their insights.

They have solid ideas, and you can build yours on theirs. Your adult children will appreciate your respect as you invite them into this collaborative effort. Just think of the confidence they gain in the implicit message that you respect their thinking and want to hear about it. Asking, "What do you think would work best?" instead of launching forth with our pearls of wisdom requires patience and the kind of respect that reminds us "it's not about me."

Remember the three perspectives from transactional analysis that we discussed in the previous chapter. It is important in its simplicity. We relate, at any point in our lives, as a Parent, as a Child, or as an Adult. We can get in touch with any of the three parts of ourselves at any moment.

The part that is activated is often in response to the actions of those around us.[2] If we pontificate as the ultimate authority, we are very much in our Parent perspective. The problem is, this encourages young adults to remain in their deferring Child perspective, while our goal is to do all we can do *to help them achieve their full maturity as adults.* When they come to us, let's set aside both our egos and that part of us that only knows how to be helpful by lecturing and instead ask ourselves: *What can best help them grow and mature as they work out this problem? How best can we facilitate their thinking maturely and creatively as we engage this decision?*

Let me be clear. When my adult children ask for my advice, I'm not shy about offering it. I am their dad and not their counselor. I try to remember—no, I really do *try*—to ask first what they think they should do. But I do love them, and often in my eagerness to be helpful, I blurt out what *I* would do. I then have the dawning awareness that I missed the step that I encourage everyone else to remember. Thank goodness I have an understanding family.

Only then, having heard their thoughts on an issue, can we give them our thoughts. There is a great chance they will have come up with some really good ideas, which we can build on. If we don't come at it the same way, we can say—respectfully, mind you—"Well, I hear you, but I see it differently."

It doesn't matter if we see the topic the same way, similarly, or totally differently; we can talk with respect. The issue in such a conversation isn't who is right or who is wrong. The issue is, *what is the wisest way to proceed?* and *how I can help my son or daughter grow in this experience of discovery?* Keep in mind that *the process* of how they think this through and engage us in it is usually as important as the solution at which they arrive.

The decision is then in their hands. We understand that. One young man told me of his appreciation on hearing his father's words, "You have to make this decision. And we will respect what you decide."

UNSOLICITED ADVICE

The greater challenge comes not when they come to us but when they don't come to us. These are the times during which we fear they are about to blunder (in our humble opinions) and we want to run their lives for them temporarily. We want to fix it! It's a judgment call, and we are questioning their judgment. Are you with me here? Of course you are. We have all been there.

So how do we respond? This is complicated. We first have to decide on which side of the line this issue resides: at one extreme, it's none of our business; at the other, they are standing on the tracks, they don't see the train coming, and this could be a disaster. The extremes are obvious, and we will come back to those. But as we move toward the middle, it gets a little more complicated. This is the gray area, and we have to decide where we draw the line. Do I keep my mouth shut, or do I bring it up? It's a judgment call.

If I overdo, either I encourage their dependency on me, or I run them away by not respecting their young adulthood, thus damaging our relationship.

If I underdo, I leave a lifetime of experience and wisdom on the table that might have been used to positive effect, thus cheating them and our relationship.

Most times, after a visit to their home, you are going to keep your mouth shut until you get in the car with your spouse, and the conversation begins, "Well, what did you think about her decision to . . ." This topic will likely not be completely exhausted when you get home. Yet you know from the days when you were there, it's their lives and their choice.

Then there are other times. You are still in the gray area, but you determine, though it's not a "big deal," it is a "deal," and you need to mention it. Often I've let issues go unspoken as Patrick and Brooke became adults, yet many times I've felt the need to tell them how I felt.

You may have an especially close relationship with your adult children, with an open invitation to express your opinion freely. Then go for it. With respect. Adult to adult. For the rest, be careful here. Many young adults with whom I speak want few of our uninvited opinions. Most will be courteous in hearing our ideas, but they may feel a quiet resentment.

"Pick your battles wisely," one young adult suggested that I advise my fellow parents. Another has said she wants to hear it "only if it is a very important issue and if I can feel free to disagree."

If it is in the gray area of importance but falls on the "I've got to bring it up" side, then *how you say it* becomes critically important. Now, you can say it any way you want to say it if you want your adult child to dread seeing you coming, but say it with respect if you want your relationship to work.

Say it with the respect you would show to a fellow adult. Think of all the times you have shared ideas—also unsolicited—with friends or colleagues at work. How did you bring it up? You brought it up with respect for their adulthood and with the awareness that they had not sought your input. Do it the same way with your adult children—though the inflection will be different because of your relationship with them and your love for them.

One litmus test I sometimes use, when I have a concern as to the level of respect I am about to show, is to ask: *what is the tone from them that I would appreciate if they were giving me input about installing an app on my iPhone or downloading software on my computer?* "Go thou and do likewise."

So what do we say? What do we say to replace statements that would begin, "Now listen, kiddo . . ."? What do we say that would communicate respect in those difficult moments when our instinct is to blurt out, "What on earth were you thinking?"

This is a loving relationship so there is no need to be formal, but there is the need to *be respectful*. Usually when the issue isn't huge you'll simply say, "Well, have you thought about . . . ?" just as you would say it to me or I to you. It's adult to adult.

Or you may begin, "When I was faced with a similar decision . . . ," or "This is what it was like for me . . . ," and then describe what you did when you were there. Or you can simply say, "Have you considered this . . . ?" These suggestions flow with the conversation and do not tell them what to do. Again, it's adult to adult and in no way controlling. Young adults today don't mind opinions—sharing theirs or hearing yours—as long as no one is telling anyone what to do.

Yet another possibility for times when you feel especially cautious is: "May I make a suggestion about that?" or "Would you like to know what I think about that?" or "May I give you some facts about this situation that I learned the hard way?" But it has to be a sincere question, which is how respect is shown. There is nothing intrusive about it. The control is entirely in their hands. The answer may be yes or no. You should respect whichever answer you get and respond accordingly.

But then there are the other times when it is a really big deal. The possible consequences and the importance of the outcome may lift this decision of theirs to a different level of importance. Whatever the issue is, the gravity of the decision and its outcome make it a really big deal. At these times, it is imperative for us to give them input they might not have considered.

Don't be shy. Say it. Still, with respect. "Son, I have to give you some input, then you can do with it as you see fit" is how I would likely put it. To me, this is said with respect—with urgency, with intensity, but still with respect. It's the same way I would voice a similar concern to a close friend in the same difficult situation.

Then in the most extreme situation, with the train bearing down on them, you'll hear from me, "Watch out!" Here I pull no punches, whether the adult relationship happens to be with an offspring of mine or not. I care, and I'm getting you off the tracks.

DAY IN, DAY OUT

Most of the time we keep quiet about their decisions and stay out of their business. They are adults. We reared them; we love them; we care about them. We want the best for them, and therefore, we know to keep our mouths shut and stay out of their way.

When we do need to speak, to give feedback, remember that rarely is there a need to be heavy-handed. A word of guidance, a tweak in direction here and there, or a bit of support from someone as important as you are to your children goes a long, long way.

My experience is, the less I say in the guidance I give, the better I am heard.

An artist friend was describing her painting to me. She paints with oils. One of the challenges, she said, is to know when the painting is completed. There is a moment in this artistic process when the work is finished, and any further strokes will diminish the beauty of the art. It is the same in giving direction to our children. There is a moment when, having said what you want to say, it is best to stop.

I was teaching a Sunday school class of young adults recently. Actually, they were teaching me. We were talking about what they need and do not need in the relationships with their parents. At the very end of the hour, as it was time to go, one of the members asked if she could add one more thought. She said, "It means the world to me to hear my parents say, 'I'm proud of you.'" There was a kind of hush in the room in the moment that followed. She had said something that resonated with everyone there.

"I'm proud of you." That's all she needed. And it meant the world.

Do you know what a "spotter" is in weight lifting? If an athlete is lying down doing a bench press, the spotter stands behind him or her, over the barbell, in case there is a need. As the athlete works to finish that set of ten reps, he or she may be struggling to get that last one completed. The spotter will reach down with no more than two fingers on each hand and apply the gentlest pressure under the bar to help, to take a slight amount of weight off. With that support, the lifter finishes the last repetition.

I was curious and talked with my friend Bill Curry who knows a bit about weight lifting. Bill has played and coached football almost all of his adult life. I asked him just how much actual weight those four fingers relieve from a bar of maybe 350 pounds. "Two," he said, "sometimes not even that much." But with the massive effort the athlete is already putting out, that's all the help he or she needs to succeed.

Your adult sons and daughters are putting out a similar effort to succeed in life. They may be almost there—so close. They may need only a little help, a word of support, someone who cares truly to listen, and a word of affirmation or guidance framed with respect. A thought or a suggestion of something they had not considered could make a difference. Who knows, it could be the two pounds that make all the difference.

"I'm proud of you." Four fingers are all that's needed. Four fingers, with God's grace, may be sufficient.

5

Good-bye, Hello

We made reservations early to make sure we could dine at our favorite restaurant. The trout there is irresistible. They always give us the huge table in the back room. The owner says it's our special place, but we know what that means. He wants us as far away from his more genteel customers as he can get us. We can get loud.

We ordered our drinks. There was a pause in all the talk. Then, out of the blue, Helen asked, "Let's have a show of hands. How many have children who have moved back home?" No one had done a head count before, and up rose a lot of hands.

There was talk and laughter about this new era with the returnees, the boomerangs. But the levity was muted as we

told our stories. "Oh, yeah, they're back home all right.
Very comfortably back home, I might add."

We tried to have fun with it. But, somehow, you could tell
this was taken more seriously than much of our foolishness.
There were questions. There were uncertainties. Who exactly
are we to each other now? Are they our kids again? Are we
roomies? Are they boarders? What does "back home" mean?
How does back home become a launching pad and not a too-
comfortable pad? And are they going to make it?

THE WORD *ADOLESCENCE* is such a part of our vocabulary
and our understanding of the developmental phases of growing up
that we can hardly imagine the term not always existing. Yet the
concept of adolescence was unheard of until the early 1900s.
Prior to that era, childhood was followed by a job and the life of
an adult. There was nothing in between.

Early in the twentieth century, the child labor laws were
changed, and secondary school became mandatory. Junior or middle high schools, which had never existed, became commonplace.
Instead of going from childhood into very young adulthood, one
went from childhood into adolescence and the next year of
school. Teenagers, no longer forced into adulthood, could engage
in the developmental tasks of adolescence.[1]

EMERGING ADULTHOOD

Some psychologists suggest that, in a similar way, the affluence
of our society has allowed a new developmental phase for our

children. They propose that for those in their twenties, the stage that now follows adolescence is "emerging adulthood" or the "odyssey years," as others have tagged it. This new phase also has given rise to the more flip references such as "twixters" and "thresholders." It is an in-between life phase that precedes full adulthood. This relatively recent occurrence is a luxury that is afforded young adults only recently and only in the most affluent societies.[2]

Emerging adulthood is one of the life stages that has been added to the traditional set of four: childhood, adolescence, adulthood, and old age. Although some would subdivide it further, most think of there now being six stages:

1. childhood,
2. adolescence,
3. emerging adulthood/odyssey,
4. adulthood,
5. active retirement,
6. and old age.[3]

Emerging adulthood is unlike adolescence in that one is expected to have a job or be pursuing graduate work in preparation for a career, but it continues some of the earlier developmental tasks of identity exploration, sorting out who one is and where one wants to invest his or her life. The first job out of school is often "just a job" and not the first step on a career path. A hallmark of this phase is the ongoing search of the direction one wants one's life to take.

Psychologist Jeffrey Arnett describes the five features of this life phase as:

1. the age of identity explorations;
2. the age of instability;
3. the most self-focused age of life;
4. the age of feeling in-between;
5. the age of possibilities.[4]

With the advent of this new phase of emerging adulthood increasingly becoming the norm, it means that young adults, though not irresponsible, don't feel the full weight of adulthood. It is a reflective, idealistic time of self-discovery with a world of possibilities before them. It is a time in which they want the advantages of a comfortable lifestyle but do not yet feel the burden of financial responsibility that comes with it. And you know what that often means: they save the expense of rent by moving back home. The popular phrases "boomerang kids" and "bungee families" came out of this pattern of emerging adulthood.

To put this in context, young adults living with their parents is hardly a new phenomenon. For the past several centuries this has been common. Sons and daughters, unless they were working as apprentices elsewhere, would live with their parents until they married. (Interestingly, until 1930, more young women lived with their parents than men, and since then—to this day—it is more men than women.) This practice peaked around the year 1940, during which a significant majority of unmarried young adults still lived with their parents.[5]

A new independence began during the time of World War II and escalated in the 1960s with these young adults increasingly living on their own after they finished school. This trend continued for several decades until it bottomed out about 2000. During the first decade of this century, young women living with their parents has increased from about 36 percent to 41 percent. For young men the pattern is the same, with slightly higher percentages.[6] This is the boomerang effect. Though the estimates vary, most say over half of college graduates will move back home with their parents for a year or two.[7] Many of those returning home are simply responding to the changing economy that has defined the past few years.

THEY'RE BACK

Robert Frost wrote, "Home is the place where, when you have to go there, they have to take you in."[8] There are many reasons our adult children want to move back in. Most reasons are financially related. They would rather have the freedom and independence of living on their own, but at this point many can't afford it. Here are some of the frequent reasons young adults want to move back home:

They graduated from college and are looking for a job.

They have a job but need to save money for the expenses of independent living.

They had a job, lost it, and can't afford to live on their own.

They are late bloomers, still developing their maturity, and can't get traction in moving forward with their lives.

They have gotten into serious debt, with student loans and credit cards, and want to save on rent in order to pay them off.

They have just gone through a personal crisis—such as a divorce, a serious illness, or rehab—and need to get back on their financial feet.

They have tried independent living and want to return to their parents' lifestyle, which they can't afford on their own.

Their reason for wanting to move back home will begin the discussion as to whether it is the best course of action. With most of the above reasons, it usually is a good decision. Often it is the only one that makes sense. The answer is yes, and soon a couple of their buddies help them load the moving truck.

So they are back. However they get there, they are back home. Here we focus not only on what is good for them but on what is good for us as well.

The first three of our touchstones are especially relevant here:

To help them move forward into this new chapter of their lives.

To help them achieve their full maturity as adults.

To establish a new, loving relationship with them.

The first two focus on *what* we are trying to facilitate and the third, *how* we are going about it. *What* we want to facilitate is their growth, and *how* we do it is respectfully and lovingly.

The time back at home can be a positive thing for their continuing maturation and growth. It gives our "emerging adults" the luxury of more time to discern and decide in what directions they want to set their sails. Lives of greater meaning and purpose can well be the result. This time together can provide the opportunity for us to help them develop abilities for engaging the challenges that lie ahead.

They may return with a feeling of personal failure. This move may be on the heels of a job loss or a divorce or some poor financial decisions. If they have feeling of inadequacy, I can think of no better place for them to return than to your care. With your help, they can learn from their failure more than from many of their successes combined. With your grace, they can heal, regain confidence, and ready themselves for the challenges ahead. This time back home can be a meaningful, healing, and positive moment in their lives.

Their return home continues your direct influence with them. *How* you structure your lives together can help shape their experiential understanding of what it is to be an adult. They can learn from you the needed skills for adulthood. Those who study these social trends already see this emerging adulthood as a healthy time of learning and reflection, producing men and women more prepared for adult life. They tend to emerge from this new phase with a clearer sense of their own identity, of who they are as adults in the world. We badly want this maturation to happen, and we know that how we engage during our time together will make a difference.

This time can be equally positive for our relationships. If this phase is well done, it can make our relationship with them even stronger as it is redefined as adult to adult. Remember that generations X and Y value relationships with family like no generation before them. They may be pills at times, but they are our pills. And they, for the most part, love us and want a good adult-to-adult relationship with us. Studies show that the best functioning young adults are those with healthy, ongoing relationships with their parents.[9]

Plan to enjoy your adult children. Let that be the self-fulfilling prophecy. This can be an especially close time for these relationships.[10] Expect it to be a positive time. Then work together to make that happen.

Our daughter, Brooke, moved back home as she looked for work following college graduation and then a year later when she was between jobs. We knew both would be temporary, and we thoroughly enjoyed the time together. As we took boxes back upstairs to her room the afternoon of her graduation, I told her, "I thought the game was over, but now we get to enjoy *overtime*." The following year she dubbed it "double overtime."

SAME HOUSE, DIFFERENT FAMILY

They are now adults—they are not returning as they left as teenagers. It's the same house and the same family, but it's a different time. They left as kids. They return as young adults.

The reality in this is as important for them to remember as it is for us. They return as young adults. For everyone's sake—especially theirs—they are expected to mature into adulthood, embracing the responsibilities that come with it.

It is often true that, when a daughter or son returns, the old patterns of what was expected of them return as well. It is only natural. The former roles we once knew are our default positions, and intuitively we may revert to them. It's time for a reset. If an adult child returns to live at home, several expectations have to change to accommodate their new adult status. This must be a conscious, joint decision in which everyone is on board. It must be done intentionally and consistently, or the old default pattern will return. *That was then, and this is now.*

This is important. When an adult son or daughter moves back in, we are a group of adults living under the same roof. All are responsible for themselves.

Let's pause at this point and recall from the second chapter that there is a tendency toward entitlement among some young adults. Not all, but some. To these, you will need to remind them it's *your* house, and they have returned because you have graciously invited them back. Mom has retired from picking up after them. She and dad have retired from paying for their sons' and daughters' former lifestyle.

The "rules of the house" will be made in consultation with them, but it is your house. Don't forget as they move back in that you have needs too. Remember the fourth touchstone:

To become more focused on this new chapter of our lives.

They lived there as children because you decided to conceive, and it was your responsibility to rear them. They live there now because you kindly invited them back, as adults, to help them out. Their first time was your responsibility. The second is your gift.

Again the touchstone, *to help them achieve their full maturity as adults*. It's now adulthood. They may be back in the house of their childhood, but they are now in their adulthood, in "the bigs" as they say in baseball. Every adult helps out—everyone pulls his or her own weight. This is to their advantage. Being responsible is a cornerstone to maturity.

I emphasize this because of the many hours I sit with counselees, who are our parental peers, and listen to their frustration. Their college graduates are back home, looking for work, and feeling as entitled as they had been allowed to feel before they left. If you, like many parents, allowed them to feel too much like the princes or the princesses in high school, then here is your chance to do it better. Use their new, fully adult status as a line of demarcation. You are all adults now. You all carry an equal load. *That was then, and this is now*.

Remember the distinction we made earlier between *caring* and *taking care of*. *Caring* means doing for our adult children what they can't do for themselves, and *taking care of* means doing for them what they can do for themselves or what they can now develop the capacity to do for themselves. The former is healthy. The latter is not, since it encourages dependency. If they can do it, back off and let them. If they should be able to do it—if they have the capacity to learn—then help them learn. If they can't do it because of whatever limitations, step in and help them.

Perhaps the best way I've heard this expressed is that we parents are to provide "a net, not a nest." As we escort them out of the nest, we always remain there for them as a supportive net for any catastrophic event or challenge beyond their ability to respond.[11]

Caring is what we now are about. We will always care for our children, but we will not be taking care of young adults who are capable of taking care of themselves.

In our staff lounge there is a sign over the lavatory, right next to the bottle of dishwashing liquid, that reads, "Unless your mama is coming by to wash your dishes, wash 'em yourself. Now." Well, Mama isn't coming by to wash the dishes.

BEGIN WITH A PLAN

So, having decided that your son or daughter is moving back, where do you go from there? Begin with a plan. No, actually begin with a serious conversation about each of your expectations, which will then result in a plan.

Ask your young adult to talk about his reasons for moving back. What does he want to achieve? How is he going to get there? How can you be helpful to him in achieving this goal? How does this goal fit with his moving back? How long does he hope to stay?

You are all working in a collaborative effort to help them with their growth, maturity, and independence. Unless they have special needs, such as a mental or physical disability, their time back home is temporary. It is a launching pad for the rest of their lives. You are more than willing to help them achieve this. Yet in doing so, you begin with the end in sight: what do they want to achieve, and how are they going to utilize the move back home to help them get there?

This "emerging adulthood" stage of their development is only a phase, not a lifestyle. It is a process. It is a phase through with they are working to get to the far side, called "adulthood." Though it may still be vaguely defined, where do they want to get, and how do they need you to help them get there?

Then talk about each of your expectations for the time they are living with you. Build that into as specific a set of agreements or mutual understandings as you feel are needed. You know your kids and their different personalities and levels of maturity. With the more mature and responsible, the "agreements" may be less formal. With those who will be looking for loopholes, you had better be pretty specific about the "rules of the house." Include household duties, hours, music (with headphones), and having guests over.[12] It is important that these are explicitly stated since there will be far less monitoring this time around.

As you talk about this game plan and work it out with them, be clear about those matters that are nonnegotiable—the ways it will be different on this second swing. If it is to be adult to adult on the respect end, it will be adult to adult on the responsibility end.

Make sure the agreed-to expectations are crystal clear.

• How will the household duties be divided up?

- Who is doing what responsibilities and when?

- Who is going to be there for dinner on what nights?

- How is it going to be communicated when plans change?

- Given that some in the house go to bed at a certain hour because they have to get up at a certain hour, then what is the understanding about when everyone is to get home?

Everybody is different, every family is different, so there is no one answer; but you have to work out *your* family's answer, be clear about it, and maintain it. Whatever is agreed to, do it. When something is left undone, it may be easier for you to go ahead and "do it myself." After all, you were about to do a load of laundry anyway. Don't do it. Follow the agreement. It's important.

The attitude being taught is *adult consideration for others*—congruent with our touchstones—and that is a great lesson they can take with them for living with any fellow adult (like maybe a spouse) the rest of their lives.

WHAT ABOUT RENT?

"Should I have them pay rent?" is another question I am asked. Of course there is no single right answer since it depends on all the factors in each unique situation. Some are pragmatic. Can they afford it? Do you need it?

The key issue is how do we structure this in a way that will help them mature and become responsible? What is best for that daughter or son always is done on a case-by-case basis. Some parents charge a token rent just as a statement of responsibility. Some teach the same responsibility by charging the full rate just as they would have to pay anywhere else. Others charge something of the going rate with the private plan of giving it back to them as seed money when they move out on their own. Still other parents have their adult children set up a savings account for themselves, put a mandatory set amount in it each month, and call it "rent."

If they are just out of college and looking for a job, you may want to welcome them back home rent-free while they look for a job. When they get a job, you can begin with a modest amount for rent. The rent can then increase in subsequent months until it reaches market value, to encourage their independence in finding their own place.[13]

Again, so much depends on the financial context of why they moved back home. If they are unemployed and you sense a lack of motivation to get a job, offer them a set number of months with free room and board. Then the rent kicks in. Still other parents start the rent at below-market value, which over time increases to above-market value as another motivation for independence.[14] Naturally, during those first months they can make "sweat payments" over and above their household duties. If your house is like most of ours, there is always plenty that needs to get done. That is a great way they can pay you when they can't afford to pay you.

The decision about rent is largely made on the basis of what makes common sense and what lessons about adult living need to be learned? Do what makes sense to help them grow. Do what will encourage them to be responsible. Do what will *help them achieve their full maturity as adults.*

Then follow through. All agreements are to be honored, both ways. If promises aren't being kept, it's time for a family meeting.

WHEN THEY GET STUCK

So they are in no hurry to move out? They have come up with an acronym for that. They are called RYAs—reluctant young adults. They are the young men and women who can't successfully make the transition into the independent life of an adult.[15] Please be clear that this is different from those who are moving forward with their lives and have a job or are pursuing graduate school, taking care of life's responsibilities—but have paused in this "emerging adulthood" phase to discern life directions, life partners, and life goals. For these reluctant young adults, there is the sense of being stuck and of getting no traction in taking on responsibilities as they make decisions.

There are many possibilities of what may be going on. It may be a lack of maturity, lack of self-confidence, lack of motivation, codependency with a parent, deer-in-the-headlights insecurity, entitlement, laziness, or simply fear of moving out and facing the challenges of independent adult life. These are different motivations but with the common result of a failure to launch.

I wrote a book on integrity titled *If You Know Who You Are, You'll Know What to Do.* A friend struggling with what to do with a failure-to-launch daughter gave me a sly smile and, after telling me he had read my book, said, "Well, Ron, I know who I am, but I still don't know what to do."

When they struggle, what do we do? Let's begin to answer that by identifying some possible origins of the problems with which they struggle. Of the numerous possibilities, I would distill them down to three groupings:

The Deer in the Headlights

The Late Bloomers

The Too Comfortable

The Deer in the Headlights: Some of these young people are virtually terrified to move out because it means moving on. They often look lazy and have a somewhat bored expression as they assure you they "have plenty of time." It's a game face to hide their fear.

They may not have even identified it as anxiety or fear—and certainly have never spoken it out loud. They may feel clammy palms as they talk of one day finding a job or their own place, but they have never identified the source of the fear. They just know it spooks them, and they want to change the subject to anything else.

Of what are they afraid? The possibilities are numerous. They may (and here we are beginning with the classic) fear failure and would rather just fear it at home than move out and prove it. Or they may fear success and the resulting increased level of expectation others would then have of them. Or they may fear the loss of the life and family they have always known. Others with a deep compassion may fear, often subconsciously, that the family might struggle without them filling their role in it.[16] Likely all who feel significant anxiety have an insecurity of their adequacy to meet life's challenges on their own.

Talk with your young adult child. Better still, first, *listen to her*, if she will talk. Spend time together. Nothing hurried, few distractions. Ask her how it feels to think of moving out. See if she will open up. It's the first step toward addressing her fears. Remember that no matter how anxious she may be, there is a part of her that wants to move forward with her life.

Having done all you can do, if she remains stuck, urge her to see a counselor.

The Late Bloomers: The best way I've heard late bloomers described is that they just need a little more runway to get liftoff.[17] We each mature at our own pace. Educators know approximately when to expect developmental milestones, but given the nature of human beings, they can never be precise. For these young adults, there isn't the sense of being stuck as much as it is simply taking longer for them to get traction.

Some move readily along hitting every marker. Others developmentally march to the beat of a different drummer. It isn't a matter of choice. They aren't resisting growing into the phase of life. It's in their wiring. They are moving at their unique pace. Remember the class picture in middle school? Some had had their growth spurt, and their skinny selves towered over the rest of us. We waited for our DNA to kick in some growth hormones. We had no choice about when it happened. Some late bloomers are similarly waiting.

The relatively new stage of "emerging adulthood" provides the extra runway they need. As young adults, they are expected to be responsible and employed, but late bloomers are excellent candidates for extra time to develop the maturity needed for the challenges and independence of adulthood.

The Too Comfortable: There are some young adults who just enjoy the comforts of (your) home too much to leave. They feel little motivation to give up the 52" flat screen and the stocked refrigerator. They know the lifestyle on their own won't come close to the one with you. With them there is no hint of emotional dependency and no sense of excessive anxiety about moving on with their lives.

Remember in an earlier chapter we focused on how we hovered over our kids, trying to catch them in mid-fall so they didn't skin their knees? Yes, too many parents made it too easy on their children. It's no surprise then, as young adults, they don't expect that to change. They just feel entitled to what they have always known.

Some call it narcissism, but that term is used a little too freely these days. Narcissism involves not only entitlement but a feeling of grandiosity as well. This is a sense that one is bigger than life, somehow more important, and therefore they are *entitled* to privileges to which the rest of us are not entitled. These young adults who are well settled into your sofa may or may not be narcissistic. They may not feel the grandiosity one bit but simply have come to expect that they will be taken care of in the manner to which they have become accustomed. They may feel *entitled* to it. They have to go.

For their sake, they need to move on. After all, a pillar of maturity is independence. Some parents increase the rent they charge these adult children. The longer they stay, the more they pay. This is a way of transitioning them into life and its costs while making life at home less and less attractive.

A time frame—okay, a *deadline*—may have to be involved. Hopefully, you can negotiate it with them. It gives them joint ownership in the decision of *when* they'll be moving even though it was clearly your idea *that* they'll be moving. Make sure the agreed-upon date is realistic in that it gives them enough time to get everything in order for the move. It can be adjusted if circumstances change. You are not trying to be punitive—you want to help them grow up. We all want this transition to be successful.

We have to give them this nudge—or perhaps a shove—because they have been misled. It was done with loving intentions, but that era of helicopter parents may have implied you would always take care of them. You won't. They have to go—for their sake.

Barry van Gerbig was a young man living in South Florida in the 1950s. He was born into a life of privilege, was the son of a Wall Street banker, and had the freedom that came with it. He was a member of Seminole Golf Club, as was the golf legend Ben Hogan. Each February, Hogan would move to Florida for several weeks in preparation for the Masters in the spring. He was compulsive in his practice routine, spending every morning on the practice tee, having lunch at noon, and playing a round of golf in the afternoon.

Barry would drive Hogan to the club in the morning and often join him for the round of golf in the afternoon. He had the luxury of setting his own schedule. A graduate of Princeton in 1961, he professionally "dabbled in this and that."

They spent much time together through the 1960s, and Hogan knew him well. One day Hogan said to him, "The things you have, this life you have, you haven't earned it. It's time for you to become your own man."

Soon after that, Barry and his wife moved to London where he got a master's degree in medical psychology and began work in the early days of the hospice movement.

It was then that he began calling Mr. Hogan "Ben."[18]

"This life you have, you haven't earned it." There is something wonderful about living the life we have earned. Karen and I remember well the early days. I had finished graduate school in pastoral counseling and was just beginning at our counseling center where I remain thirty years later. Like most professionals in a private practice structure, I experienced lean times in the early days. Because of those days, Karen and I have an appreciation for what we together have achieved and earned and enjoy.

We want the same for our children. Never do we wish them to suffer, but we do wish for them to struggle and succeed, to struggle and come out the other side with the confidence of one who has engaged the challenge and made it. Then the life they have, in all its dimensions, is the life they have earned.

6

Supporting Their New Lives

*It is now late afternoon. We are back on the porch. The valley
is before us and the mountains beyond. The sun is behind us as
we sit in the cabin's shadow. Cheese, fruit, wine, sweet tea—a
staple of the South—sit on the table. As always, we are talking.*

*We are remembering the baby shower we gave Ben and
Mary. They are the trailblazers in our group. They were the
first to have a child get married and then the first to become
grandparents. The month before their grandson was born we
surprised them with a baby shower. They were touched. We
gave them the things these new grandparents would need for
those first years of overnight visits. We laughed as we remem-
bered how awkward Ben looked as he opened gifts and acted
as if he had a clue as to what some of them were.*

They were a little older and a half step ahead of us. We were struggling to learn about being parents of adult sons and daughters. Then, suddenly it seemed, we began to be parents of married sons and daughters. We were becoming in-laws. And now some are having grandchildren. Whoa! The learning curve is getting a little steep here.

We talked of all we now had to learn. Feeling our way along. Lots of trial and error. We learn from one another— sometimes gleaning pearls of wisdom, sometimes feeling like the blind leading the blind. For each of us it often felt like we were muddling our way through, well intended to be sure, but muddling.

How do we do it now? How are we best supportive at this new place in our children's lives?

AS ADULT CHILDREN move forward with their lives they may— eventually—include marriage and they will certainly include finances. They can use our support in the former and may well turn to us for support in the latter. Marriage—how can we best be supportive without being intrusive? Finances—how can we best be supportive while promoting independence and maturity?

THEIR MARRIAGES

Remember our first touchstone? It is a simple, clear goal:

To help them move forward into this new chapter of their lives with new directions, priorities, and loyalties.

As parents, we are there to support them as they begin writing their current chapter. For many of them this may include getting married. Let me restate that. This may *eventually* include getting married. Young adults today are in no hurry to the altar. In 1970, 80 percent of Americans who were twenty-five years old had been married. Only 40 percent had been married by 2005.[1]

In part, taking longer to wed is in keeping with the bigger picture of taking their time to enjoy life and not yet take on the responsibilities that come with marriage. But there is another factor at least as important—and most positive. Remember the description of young adults from an earlier chapter? They take relationships, especially marriage and family, seriously. They want their marriages to work, and they want them to last.[2] So how do we best join them in this effort? How do we become the best advocates for their marriages we know how to be?

The success of their marriages is important. Not only the quality of their lives, but also that of our grandchildren's lives, is riding on it. Yet the quality of their relationships and the success of their marriages are not a given. Our support certainly will not guarantee their success, but it will help.

Remember the second half of our touchstone above, that this new chapter will involve *new directions, priorities, and loyalties.* Each of those three points, to a large degree, to their marriages and their families. This is their new priority. To these relationships belongs their first loyalty.

It's not about us. It's about them and whatever will best facilitate the success of these new relationships.

There is a special moment that often goes unnoticed. It happens in the wedding service, right in the middle. It is so subtle and hardly the focus of the moment. If I officiate at a wedding, it's just after I ask the groom and bride those well-known questions to which each responds, "I will." I then turn to the father of the bride, who stands between them, and ask, "And now who blesses the marriage of this woman to this man?" He speaks with clarity his well-rehearsed line, "We do" or "Her mother and I do."

Then something special happens. As all eyes are on the bride and groom joining hands, the father of the bride quietly and symbolically—here representing all four parents—*takes a backseat to the marriage.*

We step back. That's our first task in supporting their marriages. We step back so they can engage new directions, priorities, and loyalties.

If the marriage is going to work, their relationship with each other has to be top priority. In racing terms, Mom and Dad get bumped from the pole position. The newlyweds leave the sanctuary as a married couple, a new family. Their new family gets top billing over us. It is their first loyalty, and its nurture is their primary concern.

A question I usually ask couples at some point in premarital counseling is one that sounds so innocent on the face of it. I simply ask, "So, where do the two of you plan on having Thanksgiving dinner this year?"

It gets really quiet in my office. In the silence both spouses-to-be slowly turn their eyes to each other. You can tell three things in that moment. One: her mama wants them over at her house. Two: his mama wants them over at her house. Three: they have never touched this subject.

It doesn't matter to me where they have Thanksgiving dinner. They can have it at 11:30 at his mama's house and then do the mad 2:30 antacid dash to her mama's house. They can have it at their own place by themselves or invite the whole family over. It doesn't matter. It doesn't matter how they do it as long as *they* decide and base it on what is going to be good for their marriage and their new family.

As I mentioned earlier, Jesus said this so clearly: "A man shall leave his father and mother and be joined to his wife, and the two shall become one flesh" (Mark 10:7-8). I can't "become one" with someone who is number two in my life. A man and a woman leave their parents as the primary relationship in their lives in order to be emotionally available for the marriage. The marriage must come first if it is truly to be "marriage."

Naturally, this implies no disrespect to one's parents. The commandment to "honor your father and mother" is as true as ever. But one honors one's parents from a second tier, a second priority position. If the marriage is to be all that it can be, then being a husband or wife must take precedence over being a son or daughter.

It is our responsibility to understand that this is good. Difficult, perhaps. Awkward, maybe. But for a man or a woman to "leave father and mother and be joined" with each other is good and is as it should be.

HOW CAN WE HELP?

This is their new chapter. They are now married. They are trying to make a success of their marriage and their lives together. We want it to be wonderful for them. We want it to be intimate and loving. And we want to be a positive influence in this effort. So how do we do it? How do we best support the quality and success of their marriage?

Remember what you needed, and didn't need, when you were there.

Remember what you appreciated the most from your parents or in-laws and what you resented the most.

That's where I'd start.

By remembering, we bring back into focus what was really helpful from our parents and our in-laws and what was not, no matter how well intended. We remember those kind remarks from our parents and in-laws letting us know they are there for us—all we needed to do was call. Then they added that the call for help or advice was our call, not theirs. They would do everything they could not to be intrusive.

Likely what we resented the most were the times they, despite their best intentions, were intrusive. "God bless her, she is so controlling" is the way I have heard it usually expressed. (Sometimes the "God bless her" is omitted.)

One of our most important rules for the road is don't be controlling. As parents of adults, controlling is the antithesis of what we want to be if our goal is for them to grow and mature. If we are successful at controlling them—and if they have any backbone, we won't be—we have encouraged them to remain children, dependent on our wisdom and power. Implicit in this condescending message is that they are neither wise nor able to discern what is best for them. This then becomes a self-fulfilling prophecy.

If, however, we are not successful in our attempt to control them, we have sparked resentment and have done unnecessary damage in our relationship with each of them. This damage can be especially acute in the relationship with daughters-in-law and sons-in-law. They don't have the years of a loving relationship with us as a foundation to support an unfortunate remark. Regularly, over the years, I have heard a daughter-in-law say to her husband after a meal with her in-laws, "I can't believe your mother said . . ." His response is some variation of, "Aw, she was just being Mama." The daughter-in-law didn't grow up with her, so she wasn't "just being Mama" to her.

I also understand the challenge a family is given when a young man or woman marries into their fold. A foreigner has arrived. This new person has a different background, different traditions, and different expectations of what "family" means. This person won't keep the house, parent the children, or even decorate the tree as we always have done it. This may take some getting used to when we visit. This can be a challenge. "What on earth is she thinking?" may come to mind on occasion.

It can be difficult keeping quiet in these moments—especially when they have children and are parenting differently than you would. But as a friend of mine said referring to a time when she wisely kept her counsel to herself, "I just had to put on my big-girl britches and deal with it."

She happens to be married to your son, but it is their family and their lives. Not yours. Unless they are endangering your precious grandchildren or you see disaster written all over the direction they are taking, put on your big-girl or big-boy britches and keep it to yourself.

All these cautions notwithstanding, I am rather high on in-law relationships. My experience continues to confirm they usually are quite wonderful. We become "like family" to one another, and then we become family. The DNA line blurs. We are all family, when it goes well. And it goes well, in part, because of good relational chemistry and, in part, because of what we each do to respect and nurture the relationship we are given.

I also find boomer parents have little about which to be critical of their son's or daughter's parenting. There is not much we have to "keep to ourselves." These young adults tend to be excellent parents. They are loving and personally involved in their children's lives. They are intentional about what they are doing as parents, how they are doing it, and its effect on their children. I know a lot of young parents and am pleased to report that our grandchildren are in good hands.

DADS GETTING IN THE GAME

Dads often struggle to be personal with their adult children. You don't have to become someone you're not in doing this. Most dads I know care deeply, and many can translate that into an equally deep conversation with their sons and daughters. Fathers today, in fact, connect more personally than any generation before them. Some, however, carry the burden of their fathers, many of whom couldn't say "I love you" though it was clearly true. This may have been a loss in the relationships with our dads, but it doesn't have to be for our children.

Many of us dads let our wives carry the ball in the relationship and conversations with our children. It then continues into their adult lives. One of them will call home, Dad answers, and far too soon he says, "Well, here's your mom." She then catches him up on what is going on with the children and the grandchildren after the conversation is over. A part of this hesitancy, of course, is that moms are pros at this relationship stuff, and dads feel like rank amateurs. My wife is one of those pros. She and our daughter have the most wonderful conversations—sometimes just catching up and at times plowing deeply.

I remember one time, when our daughter, Brooke, was still away at college, I wanted to be intentional about getting more involved in her calls back home. It was the Sunday afternoon after her spring formal. She called, and I happened to answer. I asked her every question I possibly could think of to ask about the evening and the dance. I asked about her date, her dress, and even her shoes! For a male, it was impressive. As I told a buddy the next day, "There was absolutely no question left unasked." Then I gave the phone to Brooke's mom. God as my witness, they talked for at least half an hour with virtually no backtracking over terrain Brooke and I had covered. In a thousand years I never would have thought of asking her about the color of her roommate's dress. I was in awe of their relationship.

Dads, most of us will not have that kind of relationship. Some do, and I try to contain my envy. But most don't. That doesn't mean that we can't sincerely check in at a more personal level. And ask. And want to know. And listen.

A SUBTLE DEMOTION

Please don't wait until they are married to promote them to full adult status. It often happens. They are, to some degree, treated as kids until their wedding. Then a new level of respect kicks in.

For instance, I may be talking with the eldest of three young adult sisters. Let's call her Mary. She is in her early thirties and single. Her middle sister married three years ago, and baby sis had her wedding last summer. Mary has noticed something unusual in these past few months. She feels demoted. No, that's not quite right. It's more like her sisters have been *promoted* over her.

She noticed it at the holidays. Their parents consulted each of the married daughters as to the dates that would be best for their schedules before any plans were made. These plans were then announced to Mary. It was such a simple thing. Small, really. But it was symbolic. It was noticed. And it hurt.

All of this happened before the bedroom accommodations were assigned, and, of course, Mary got the pullout sofa in the sunroom.

We understand it. In some ways parents are going out of their way to show respect for their new daughters-in-law and sons-in-law. They want to be gracious and develop a positive relationship. Plus, they are trying also to accommodate the in-law family's schedule.

Yet in a subtle, subconscious way, Mary hasn't graduated into full adult life. The married daughters are *consulted*. Mary is *told*. Marriage is one of those implicit milestones—such as being financially independent or having children. Then you're *really* an adult.

Mary's parents would never want to offend her. But unless they are intentional, they may communicate that Mary doesn't have to be taken seriously as a full adult—yet.

It is positive to know that married daughters and sons are given their due respect as adults, yet we must guard against letting marriage be a line of demarcation between adulthood and something less than full adult status.

FINANCIAL RESPONSIBILITY

We must talk about finances. Our sons and daughters often turn to us for money. In virtually every decision we make regarding our financial interaction with them, let our touchstone be at least in the background: How can you help them grow into their full maturity? How can you help them take responsibility for their lives and make consistently wise decisions?

Our young adult sons and daughters have grown up and graduated into an awful economy. Professional prospects currently are bleak. Jobs are scarce. Pay is less. Only half of the jobs that college graduates fill require college degrees.[3] And they often are in debt way over their heads. The student loans were bad enough, but now those credit cards—that looked like such a good idea to get—are about maxed out. Oh, and then there is the interest rate on them.

New graduates currently leave college with an average of $24,000 in student loans and $4,100 in credit card debt.[4] Many are in a hole that will take years to escape.

So here comes the question. You saw it coming, right? Should we help them pay off the debt they built up? Please don't reach for the checkbook too quickly. Ask, talk, think, and discern the wisest decision based on our touchstone, our goals for this phase. Take your time. Then, whether you decide to give money or advice, remember they are under stress, so do it with compassion. Let them know you care during this difficult time. But, first, focus on the proper questions.

How did they get in this financial hole? Were they working hard and being responsible, but student loans simply mounted? Or were they less than responsible and lived a lifestyle they couldn't afford, ignoring the debt? How can this moment, this decision, help them learn and become more financially mature? What can they learn about responsible spending and the consequences of excessive borrowing—while not drowning in an ocean of debt that is beyond their means?

This situation makes financial advisors nervous. Immediately they will caution you never to give away money that may be required for your own financial security. What you have saved for retirement, they will tell you, must be kept for retirement. And they are right. There are some tragic stories out there about very poor elderly parents and grandparents who, with the finest intentions, made unwise decisions.

Let's assume you have the resources to pay off their debt without any risk to your financial position. Should you? It's such a judgment call even as you have our goals of their "full maturity" and "moving ahead" in sight. How you respond has a lot to do with the issues of how they got in this situation and what are their attitude and maturity level regarding finances. You will want to be far more generous if they have been financially sensible and hard-working, but circumstances, plus student loans, overwhelmed them. In other words, they have the maturity, so there aren't major lessons of responsibility to be learned by how you handle this.

If they have been irresponsible in their spending and you readily bail them out, what have they learned? They have learned that if they are irresponsible in their spending, you will readily bail them out, which is not a lesson that will move them toward the maturity we were talking about.

Instead, why not, with compassion and support, help them figure out what they are going to do with their problem. Teach them the things they don't know how to do. Help them restructure their debt to make the payments manageable and get them out from under those horrific credit card interest rates. Help them explore repayment options for any student loans. Help them work out a budget so they can live within their means.

You may feel yours is a situation in which more than advice and counsel is called for. You may feel it is wise to pay all or a portion of their indebtedness. Then be intentional in *how* you do it.

Let's say you determine there is no way they can pay off all the debt themselves in any time frame that would allow them to move forward with their lives. If you are going to pay it off, make sure they know this is a "once in a lifetime" gift that will never be duplicated under similar circumstances. Encourage them to take whatever steps are needed to get their financial house in order. "Believe me," I'd say, "this is once in a lifetime."

Or perhaps you feel that their paying a portion of the debt would be sufficient to teach them the lessons in responsibility. Then *match* their payments. For every dollar they pay toward their debt, you match it. Or for every two they pay, you pay one—whatever the agreed upon ratio.

This way they feel the pressure, the consequence of their spending what they hadn't earned, without being hopelessly overwhelmed. We'll let them sink. We won't let them drown.

After helping them out of their financial hole, encourage them to gain the skills and insight to avoid new debt. Make them aware of educational resources from which they can learn about budgets, 401(k) plans, savings, emergency funds, and responsible money management. Offer to be one of those resources, if they like. They may take you up on it.

MEDICAL INSURANCE

Be sure that all your children, of any age, have medical insurance. This is not an issue of "whatever will best help them learn and grow." If they are not covered and are diagnosed with a devastating illness, it could ruin you financially. You should do whatever it takes to get the medical care your children need. Without insurance, it can only come out of your pocket. Here we turn to our fourth touchstone about your moving into *this new chapter of our lives*. If you are wiped out financially, you won't have much of one.

They likely can be included on your policy if they are under the age of twenty-six. If they are older, you can get a catastrophic policy with a high deductible for just such unlikely, but possible, events. They need it, and *you* need them to have it.

DO NOT MAKE YOURSELF VULNERABLE

Do not do anything for your children (or anyone else) that might ruin you financially. Do not cosign any loan that you cannot easily afford to pay off. Be reluctant to cosign for a credit card with adult children. If they do not make timely payments, it could ruin your credit rating. If they max the card out, you are legally just as responsible as they are to pay. It is sobering to know that three-quarters of cosigned loans are eventually paid off by the cosigners.[5]

Do not do anything that would make you vulnerable financially. Should you find that you are tempted to do just that—

should you find that you tend to say yes when your best instincts are shouting no, then do some serious reflecting on that. What are you getting by saying yes?

This is the classic "caretaker" dynamic: to do for others at the sacrifice or risk of one's own welfare. I have known of aging parents who cosigned a large loan for their sons to begin a risky business venture. "I just couldn't tell Henry no" is the terribly sad lament of these fine people who now face financial devastation.

If I can't "tell Henry no," then *I have a serious problem.* Don't even think about telling me it's "Christian" or "loving." It's a dependency on something—likely Henry's approval. It may be based in a self-esteem issue that I need to do for others because subconsciously I don't feel I bring as much to the relationship as they do. It may be based on the fear that if I don't do what Henry wants, he won't be coming around. If so, then the relationship is not based on love, and that needs to be addressed.

You must deal with your reluctance to stand for what you know is right for you. And while you are dealing with it, go ahead and say no. Establish healthy boundaries of how far you are willing to go to help others out and not violate your own boundaries.

If your children come to you with a request that would make you vulnerable, as you turn them down, remind them that you are doing them a favor. If you were financially ruined, they would have to take care of you in your old age.

Each time your adult children turn to you, you want to be responsive. Remember that that does not necessarily involve a checkbook. Guidance and wisdom may be the most substantial gifts you could ever offer.

7

Dealing with the Difficult Times

It is getting to be late in the evening. What a wonderful day it has been. We all sit together in front of the fireplace. The logs that were blazing are now glowing embers. No need to throw on another one. We'll all be turning in soon. The wine glasses are empty. The cups of hot tea are cold. What had been an animated conversation on important issues— like, well, college football—has become more subdued.

Like the fire, the passion has subsided from our voices. We begin catching up on any yet untold details of our families. We're talking mainly of our children again, and truth be told, we have gone to bragging. But no one ever minds since we all want to know and are eager to celebrate together.

No one seems to have noticed—or at least mentioned it—that Bob and Judy have been quiet through much of the evening. In fact, as I later recalled, they had been more subdued through the weekend. That is not the norm, especially for Judy.

They remain quiet as the talk continues around them.

"Now, everyone, you can't tell this to a soul, but it looks like young Randy is going to make partner this fall," we hear from his proud mom. Randy is like a nephew to most of us, and we each swell a little. Congratulations to Nancy and Rob are heard from around the room. Then we settle back into a moment of silence.

We stare sleepily at the dimming glow of the fireplace. In the growing darkness, no one sees the tear as it slowly eases its way down Judy's cheek.

IT HAS BEEN SAID that "parents are as happy as their unhappiest child." This can be painfully true.

We have all dreamed of our ideal scenario, in which our children grow and mature, get their educations, get jobs, perhaps get married, and move on with their lives. It's neat, and it's relatively simple—and a lot easier said than done. Again, it's like our metaphor of a delicate mobile having achieved its balance. The mobile of the family is in balance—all is well.

And then—*boom*—a piece drops off. Something big happens to an adult son or daughter.

A job is terminated.

A marriage ends.

A spot on the MRI looks suspicious.

A child is born. "But," the doctor says, "I'm afraid there are problems."

Maybe we learn from our son's wife that he is struggling with alcohol or depression.

Or a daughter calls at 2:30 in the morning from a battered women's shelter.

A piece drops off or a new one is added or a terrible blow is inflicted onto our delicate mobile.

When they struggle—and there will be times our children will struggle—what do we do? Of course, it depends on many variables:

the nature, the severity of the struggle

their ability to handle it themselves

resources already available to them

the dynamics of our relationship with them

their attitude toward receiving help, and so on and on...

Then we have to decide *how* we best respond—from one extreme of letting them handle it themselves to the other extreme of taking charge. There are far too many variables to have simple answers here. So the question becomes, What are the touchstones? By what measures do we decide?

Remember our goals in being parents of young adults. The first two focused on our hopes for them:

To help them move forward into this new chapter of their lives.

To help them achieve their full maturity as adults.

Those are our touchstones. Those are our measures by which we base any decision. What do we do? is the question we ask ourselves when they face such a need or crisis. Do we stand back, respecting their adulthood, allowing them to gain more maturity and confidence? Or is this challenge too great for their current ability, and we help them "move forward" with an assist? Or do we respond with something in between?

Remember the touchstones. If we know what we are about, we'll be aimed in the right direction of what to do.

What is best going to achieve those goals of maturity, character, and moving successfully into adulthood? Do we let them work it out, or do we intervene?

How do we address the topic while helping them grow? How do we intervene with this problem, join them in this crisis while respecting their adulthood, and encourage their independence?

Sometimes the accent comes down on one side. Sometimes on the other side. It depends on the nature of the crisis and the severity of the danger.

The debate goes on in our minds. The decision often isn't easy. Letting them work it out has the advantage of giving them the confidence in their own abilities to address difficult issues. It helps achieve those important elements of maturity: independence and self-sufficiency.

Then, in other contexts, such as drug addiction or major depression, if we sit back to let them work it out, we would be sitting back and watching the lives of those we love crash and burn. No, when they can't help themselves, we intervene. It's not intrusive. It's not disrespectful. It's loving.

We will briefly consider four especially difficult situations with which your adult child could be faced: substance abuse, mental illness, developmental disability, and lifestyle differences. As you address any critical situation with your adult child, get the professional help and guidance you will need to respond most appropriately. My focus in this chapter is not the specifics of what you will need to do, but—in the spirit of our previous chapters—helping you decide when to intervene and how to become involved while still respecting the adults they have now become. My task here is to highlight the basis on which our decisions are made. You will have to discern the specific details and make the final call.

In each of these, remember our touchstones—how can we help them achieve their full maturity and successfully move ahead in this new chapter of their lives?

WHEN THEY ARE DEALING WITH SUBSTANCE ABUSE

We pull out all the stops. We do whatever it takes to get them the help they need. If they are married, we work closely with the spouse. The marriage partner takes the lead, but we stand ready to be active members of the team. If they are not married, we take charge. We get them help. "As God is my witness," we whisper to ourselves, "I will move heaven and earth to get him the help he needs."

Addiction means they are no longer at the controls. They are no longer in charge of their lives or their choices. So your intervention—perhaps literally—is not intrusive; it's compassionate. You would deal with this crisis in their lives just as you would for any other adult in your family in the same situation. You would intervene with a spouse, a parent, or a sibling. You would intervene with an adult child.

I referred earlier to the distinction between *caring*, doing for people what they cannot do for themselves, and *taking care of*, doing for people what they can or should be able to do for themselves. At the heart of alcohol or drug addiction is chemical dependency. If your son or daughter is actively addicted, then he or she likely cannot achieve sobriety for or by himself or herself. Your intervention not only is caring but also may be lifesaving.

I have a friend—let's call him Richard—whose brother was an alcoholic and was addicted to illegal drugs and sometimes was homeless. The brother lived in a distant city, geographically beyond my friend's ability to make a significant difference in his life. He lived with the awareness that his brother was wasting away from the addictions and the elements.

Richard had to do something. It's what families do. Their father was elderly and no longer had the capacity or insight to intervene for his son, so Richard stepped in for him. He called his dad. He said if they didn't do something soon he would outlive his younger son. It was arranged. Much of what would be the brother's inheritance was given to Richard in a trust for his brother's care.

He drove out West, packed the car, and brought his brother back to live closer to him. To find him a place to live and work to do was the only thing that had integrity for him. Richard's brother—a man weathered well beyond his years—now had a clean apartment, a car, and a job. It's what families do. They care for one another.

Life is real and not a fairy tale. This story does not conclude with everyone living happily ever after. Richard's younger brother continued to struggle with health issues from a hard life, lived several more years, and died before his time. But his final years were lived in safety, with dignity, and near a brother who cared.

That is what we do as families. We care.

As the parents of our adult children, we may find ourselves in the same role that Richard had adopted. If we are convinced that our adult child has an addiction to alcohol or any drug, we take action. Again, we are not overriding her adulthood. A chemical substance has already overridden the maturity and judgment of her adulthood. Because of her addiction, she no longer is in charge of her life. We will indeed be intrusive, not in disrespect of her adulthood, but to return her to adulthood—in respect of the reality that a substance beyond her is now in control.

So what do you do?

Let's say it's your son who is addicted to either alcohol or drugs. If he is married, then hopefully you can work hand in hand with his spouse in getting him evaluated and into treatment. She will likely welcome your support with open arms. She loves him as well and, after all, is living with this problem "up close and personal" daily. (Now, there is always the chance she doesn't agree with you. Should you be concerned about your son in ways that his wife does not share, seek professional help to get an objective opinion as to who is more accurate in his or her assessment.)

If he is not married, you take the lead in getting him professional help. Let's first assume he agrees with you about his addiction. Then get him to a therapist who specializes in addiction. Let me emphasize the need to see a specialist in this field. Deceit and deception become a part of the personality of everyone who is addicted. This requires a therapist who knows the drill, can discern the truth from a lie, and can provide the help required. The therapist will give you an evaluation as to your adult child's level of need: attending AA meetings, AA meetings with therapy, an outpatient treatment program at a clinical setting, or inpatient treatment. More treatment is better than less, but let your son begin at whatever level of treatment he is willing to engage. If it doesn't work, he can move up to a more intense level of help.

As he begins his treatment, you go to Al-Anon meetings. Attend several. Listen. Learn. Ask questions. Colleagues of mine who specialize in this area say to make sure you find meetings with other parents—their needs and perspectives differ somewhat from those of spouses. You need to learn what is supportive and what is enabling. You need to learn what is helpful and where boundaries need to be set. Don't be shy about attending these.

They are good. If, for any reason, you don't feel comfortable at the Al-Anon group you are attending, try another group.

Now, I began with the easier of the two possibilities—he agrees that he has a problem. And he may. But don't be surprised if he balks.

Denial is frequently a part of any addiction. He can look you right in the eye and say he doesn't have a problem. He may believe what he is saying. It's simply denial. In his own mind he is being perfectly honest; it just may not be true. Or he may know he's lying. It doesn't make him a bad person; lying comes with the turf of addiction. The addiction has taken over. Deceit and dishonesty become tools to keep the addiction going. As I heard a long-standing recovering alcoholic say, "Heck, we lie just to keep in practice."

If he will not get help, then you attend the Al-Anon meetings and/or make the appointment with the therapist for yourself to get a consultation on how best to proceed. Again, find a therapist who specializes in addictions and, if your son is in denial, one who directs interventions. Spell out to the therapist what you know about his situation to get the professional feedback you need on the severity of the problem. Then if you are correct that this is alcoholism or drug addiction, you will be advised on how to proceed. You may well begin working with the therapist on structuring an intervention.

Please know that interventions are often effective. For someone with a serious chemical dependency, it is a powerful moment to sit with six to eight of the most important people in his life—and from each area of his life—and hear the same message of concern. He can deny it if he hears it from one or even two. It's hard to say something isn't true when the vote is unanimous, especially from those whose investment is in nothing but their care for him. You, of course, will want to participate in this meeting.

There are two types of interventions. The traditional type is the surprise or "ambush" type, in which the person walks into an arranged meeting with several friends and family members who tell him of their concern and encourage him to get treatment. He is unaware of what is about to happen until he walks into the room. A second type is known as an "invitational intervention," in which your son, along with the family, is invited to an educational meeting or workshop. The intent is to help him learn about the disease of addiction and the treatment available. The advantage to this intervention is the respect that is shown—thus avoiding the anger and resentment of feeling like the victim of a surprise attack.

The therapist will lead you through this process. He or she will guide you in structuring the intervention, lead the meeting, and take your son to a treatment facility if the intervention has been successful and your son is willing to go.

As parents, you will want to facilitate getting him into treatment. You will then support him in whatever way the professionals advise you during treatment and beyond as he gets back on his feet. But during this recovery process, your role is increasingly toward the background. You were intentionally intrusive—and appropriately so—when the alcohol or drug had taken charge of his life. Now that he is taking control again, you resume your place in his adult life. You will be supportive and helpful in any appropriate way, but you will not be in charge.

WHEN THEY MAY BE SUFFERING
FROM A MENTAL ILLNESS

Parents tend to know their children like no one else. Unless they have been married a while, you instinctively know them the best. You can smell when something isn't right. You don't have to know the nine symptoms of depression or the nuances of the mood swings of bipolar disorder to know that "Jonathan just isn't Jonathan."

So much of what I wrote in the previous section about addiction applies here. If your adult child is mentally ill, you will join with his or her spouse in getting the professional help needed. If your son or daughter is not married, you take the lead. Again, this is not disrespectful of his or her adulthood. You would intervene as much as you would if it were a spouse, a parent, or a close friend.

But with mental illness we are swimming in murkier waters. How people are doing emotionally and how they "seem" are often ambiguous and hardly black and white. Mental or emotional problems may not be easily identified, and the lines are not clearly drawn. At what point on the continuum of depression do you press your concern? At one end, they seem unusually down or blue; at the other, they can't make themselves get out of bed in the morning.

Since emotional lives are lived in the subjective gray, you may get disagreement about the severity of the problem. As with issues of substance abuse, you may get resistance. Yet unlike denial of substance abuse, most people aren't into denial about feeling lousy. If they are depressed or anxious or find their emotions swinging to the extremes, they often want it addressed as well. They may disagree about how serious it is—and don't want to be labeled—but want to feel better and often are willing to get help.

If you believe something is going wrong emotionally, trust your instincts, and do your best to hold up to them the mirror of what you see in them. Do it clearly, directly, and supportively.

We are not picking on our adult children here. If we saw unhealthy emotional signals in anyone we loved, we would have the same concern. And we would similarly bring that concern to his or her attention.

Mental illness refers to a broad range of dynamics in which one's emotions, thinking, and resulting behaviors become affected. You will sense a change in mood in someone beginning to struggle. This becomes an "illness" when it lessens one's core sense of well-being and affects the ability to function on the job and in relationships. Quality of life has become significantly disrupted and impaired. At the extreme we sense a concern that one might be self-destructive or suicidal.

Before you get overly concerned, consider the context at this moment of their lives. They may be dealing with an issue in which heightened anxiety is a normal and healthy response. Or they may be working through a dilemma requiring their attention, focus, and emotional energy—leaving them temporarily with the same symptoms as depression. The problem may not be with their emotional state but with the dilemma they are facing.

At other times there is reason for concern about their mental health. Details of the diagnosis of mental disorders are beyond the scope of this writing, but the specifics are not what we need anyway. That's why mental health professionals are there. The signs and symptoms are what we want to notice.

So what are the signs? Pay special attention to increased depression, anxiety, or unusual mood swings. This is where parents and spouses have a big advantage. They know the baseline. They know when he is "being Jonathan" and when he isn't—when there is something wrong. Note if you see any significant change in Jonathan's mood or actions that feels unhealthy, especially toward depression or anxiety.

If you begin to get an uneasy feeling that your adult child is depressed, here is the list of symptoms to look for according to the National Institute of Mental Health. Anyone who is depressed will likely have a majority of these:

- Persistent sad, anxious, or "empty" feelings

- Feelings of hopelessness and/or pessimism

- Feelings of guilt, worthlessness, and/or helplessness

- Irritability AND restlessness

- Loss of interest in activities or hobbies once pleasurable, including sex

- Fatigue and decreased energy

- Difficulty concentrating, remembering details, and making decisions

- Insomnia, early-morning wakefulness, or excessive sleeping

- Overeating or appetite loss

- Thoughts of suicide OR suicide attempts

- Persistent aches or pains, headaches, cramps, or digestive problems that do not ease even with treatment[1]

If your concern is more toward anxiety, here are some of the common symptoms. Please understand, though, that "anxiety" covers a broad range of conditions from generalized anxiety to panic attacks to obsessive-compulsiveness. Some symptoms often associated with anxiety are:

- Excessive worry about events, situations, or problems

- Difficulty concentrating

- Feelings of tension or restlessness and often keyed up

- Irritability

- Muscle tension

- Sleep difficulties

- Inability to refocus from concerns

- Panic attacks of intense fear

Beyond depression and anxiety, your son or daughter could be dealing with the mood swings of bipolar disorder, a personality disorder, or even schizophrenia. All of these must be taken seriously and addressed readily.

You may have noticed that my focus is not on specific diagnoses. Our job is not diagnosing but providing help when needed. When you are concerned, don't turn to the Internet to find the appropriate diagnostic category. It is terribly complex, and many symptoms overlap.

You are the pro at knowing when something isn't right. You're not the pro at the diagnosis and treatment. Even if you are right about a diagnostic category, your son or daughter may feel labeled and may shut down if you identify him or her with a personality or mood disorder. Being told one is "clinically depressed" or "bipolar" may offend, and up will go one's defensive walls. It will be heard as an accusation. In the conversation expressing your concern, simply share the changes you have seen out of the love you have for him or her. Present the facts. "It deeply concerns your mom and me when we see . . . " is the way I would begin. Then get excellent help.

Feel blessed that we live in the era in which most mental health issues can be successfully addressed. Therapy—and medication when needed usually results in those who struggle being able to lead healthy and meaningful lives.

If you would like more information on mental illness or directories for therapists, research the following organizations:

- American Psychological Association

- American Psychiatric Association

- American Association for Marriage and Family Therapy

- American Association of Pastoral Counselors

WHEN THEY HAVE A DEVELOPMENTAL DISABILITY

Being the parent of a developmentally disabled child is a delicate balance between creating a safe world in which he or she will live and respecting the freedoms of his or her adulthood within that world.

If our adult children are able and healthy, we set them free to live their lives. If there is a disability inhibiting them from functioning independently, we provide them the care they will need in response to their inability to care for themselves.

Developmental disabilities are chronic conditions by which one may be affected both mentally and physically. Among the best known of these disabilities are cerebral palsy, intellectual disability, and autism spectrum disorders. Each condition will last throughout the person's life. It may affect her learning, mobility, language, and ability to live independently.[2] As a special-needs child matures into adulthood, her parents will always keep one eye to the future.

Let's call her Amanda. When Amanda was born, her parents heard the words that cut to their hearts: "but there are problems." The shock first stunned them, and then they were overtaken by hurt, disappointment, and concern.

In the weeks that followed they were able to take it in. Their caring physician guided them to groups, websites, and other useful resources. Slowly at first, then with a passion, they learned thoroughly what Amanda's condition involved and what it would mean in her life. They learned of her impairments and her disabilities. They took it in and digested it. There were moments of profound sadness. They thought of all the dreams they would have to replace. With the resiliency of loving parents, they renewed their focus on Amanda and what she would need.

The years went by, and Amanda grew. The disabilities they expected became increasingly apparent. She is now a young woman. Long ago they worked through the emotional challenges and came to an acceptance of their reality. They would never be "letting go" of Amanda as they had their other children. Amanda's brother and sister are now grown and living on their own. She, too, is in her midtwenties but is still at home, where she will stay. With that eye toward the future, her parents began planning when she was still a child for her care should she outlive them.

Parents whose children have developmental disabilities will be involved with their care for the rest of their lives, more or less, depending on the level of need. So how does the idea of respecting their adulthood come in? Here I draw a distinction between their independence and their adulthood. Their parents recognize their need for dependence on others while they honor their adulthood.

Their adult children are given their independence to the degree they have the ability to make mature decisions and to live independently. Cognitive limitations will impair some in thinking through issues and coming to sound judgments. Physical limitations will affect the mobility of others to live on their own. Still others, who are affected by both limitations, will have their options further narrowed. Yet their manhood and womanhood continue to be honored.

These special-needs young adults are treated with the respect and dignity that adulthood brings, just as we are treated with respect and dignity. We all have limitations. There is no correlation between limitations and respect.

To the degree that is appropriate, their parents will help them understand their limitations and how those limitations will affect the way they live their lives. Parents will respond to questions about getting married, having children, or going to college in thoughtful and sensitive ways. Parents nurture their special-needs adults with care as they develop an understanding of their self-identity.

I have learned from parents who have developmentally disabled children how to relate with a respect for their adulthood. Their children are encouraged to develop themselves and their abilities, to become as fully functioning adults as they can be—which is the effort of every parent of every child. In respecting their adulthood, parents want their children to become as independent adults as they have the capacity to become. They also consult with their adult children and engage them in the process of making decisions for their lives, to the degree that this is appropriate.

These special-needs adults will always remain—either directly or indirectly—under the care of a family member. Many will remain at home until it is in their best interest to live in a group home or until their parents' age or limitations make it necessary. Others will move in with adult siblings.

It is a challenge to be the parents of a special-needs child, but it once was more isolating. Today, thanks to the Internet, there are virtual communities and face-to-face communities providing information, resources, and vital support.

The goal remains the same: to help them achieve their full maturity as adults in this new chapter of their lives. Long ago parents of special-needs adults intuitively reset the bar on what full maturity and its resulting independence would mean. Parents want, expect, and work to facilitate their children becoming all that they can be as young adults. Parents work throughout their children's childhood and adolescence—through education, physical therapies, training, workshops—to help them achieve the full measure of their abilities in their adult lives.

WHEN THEY HAVE LIFESTYLES THAT DIFFER FROM OUR VALUES

So what do you do when your adult children lead a lifestyle that differs from your own and from your personal values? Remember our third goal.

To establish a new, loving relationship with them—adult to adult—with mutual respect and appropriate boundaries.

"Loving relationship." "Adult to adult." "Mutual respect." All of that is relatively easy until we disagree with our adult children, especially when we disagree on values and life philosophies. They are now adults. We have every right to be heard but with no authority to direct them. If the conversation over a "value" issue is to conclude with the relationship intact, it must be engaged with mutual respect of each other's perspective and adulthood. You have to respect your young adult's perspective as he or she has to respect yours.

What if your twenty-eight-year-old daughter wants to move in with her boyfriend? She is an adult and independently making her own way in life. Let's assume that for you, an unmarried couple cohabitating is morally wrong. Even though some parents have no problem with it, for others, cohabitation is a serious moral problem and is in contrast with their belief system and their faith.

She informs you of her plans in an e-mail. You can just feel your internal pot quickly coming to a boil. There has to be a conversation or the lid could blow off the relationship. Tell her of your need to talk with her about it. Face-to-face, of course. No e-mail. No phone. This is a real relationship, and the important matters always deserve a face-to-face conversation.

First, listen. Ask about her perspective. Make no assumptions. Get to know where she is in her thinking, so you can understand her and her perspective. Take her as seriously as you want to be taken. There is one other reason to listen carefully. If you want to be heard, you begin by hearing.

Then try to be heard and understood. Tell her how you feel morally, ethically, and theologically. Talk with her. Be succinct. The fewer words you use, the more likely you will be heard. Don't try to ram your view down her throat. This isn't a debate. Remember, mutual respect. Her view is just as important to her as yours is to you. Don't be dictatorial. It always backfires. The answer "because I said so" long ago became irrelevant.

Have an open exchange of ideas. Each of you should talk about your reasons, your perspectives, and your values. Hopefully, this open exchange was already a permanent part of the relationship.

Having expressed your view, you then have to turn it over to her. You have no authority over her choices. That ship has sailed. You then pray for the best.

There is one question that always arises regarding cohabitation. If she and her boyfriend live out of town and come to visit, what should the sleeping arrangements be? It's your house, and it's your rules—just like it's their rules at their house. You can't abandon your values, or you will lose your integrity. You are not forcing your values on them. You are honoring what you believe in your own home. If this means they want to stay in a hotel, respect their decision. There is no reason for anyone to be offended. They are honoring what they believe, just as you are. Tell them you understand and that breakfast will be ready when they get there.

You may have to engage just such lifestyle and moral issues. Some may be more serious than others. Please remember, as you maintain the integrity of your moral stance, there is precious little that is more important than the loving relationship with your daughter.

Even if you disagree, you must not let these moral issues permanently rupture the relationship. If you do, you may not only lose the relationship but also lose the positive moral influence you could have for years to come.

Stay in the relationship. Respect her. Disagree with her. But always love her and stay connected with her.

The relationship itself is more valuable than any issue that will arise. As writer Anthony Brandt said, "Other things may change us, but we start and end with family."

Then there is another challenging situation with which parents sometimes are faced. Let's say a set of parents have an adult son who has announced to them that he is gay. For parents who believe homosexuality is a choice, this is a values issue. For those who believe homosexuality is in the DNA, it is a lifestyle issue. For almost all parents, their response likely will be shock. It's an announcement many parents don't see coming.

Should it happen, please know that your son has probably been dreading talking with you for years. This has taken all the courage he could muster. And finally he is there. Try to set aside your shock and your disappointment at the dreams you had that will never to be realized and remember, as best you can, that he is asking one thing and one thing only: "Do you still love me?"

As you give him the supportive hug of a lifetime, tell him, "I will always love you." In the moment, this is all that matters. You will work out the rest later. Later you will get to know this part of his life, and he will get to know how you feel. There will be plenty of time for those conversations.

Do not allow this moment to define, much less ruin, the relationship.

In that moment, it doesn't matter what our philosophy or theology of human sexuality is.

It doesn't matter how much we may have thought it through or understand it.

It doesn't matter if we agree with him or not.

In the moment, that is not the issue.

Remember the *topic* may be human sexuality, but the *issue* is, "Do you still love me?" And the answer is yes.

You will then get to know him as you have not known him before. In multiple conversations he will talk of his loneliness and his sadness, of his fear of discovery and his fear of rejection. In those same conversations you will talk of your feelings and your thoughts about homosexuality. You will get to know each other anew.

There are different theories about homosexuality. Essentially the debate is between nature versus nurture. Is it in the genetic DNA, or is it a result of one's childhood years? That discussion is beyond the focus of this book. I am writing about how we relate with our adult children, not how our adult children became who they are.

My consistent experience is that, whatever the origin of one's sexual preference, by the time he reaches adulthood, sexual orientation rarely ever changes. Straight or gay, it's likely not going to change. I have talked with many parents whose son or daughter has told them he or she is gay or lesbian. Most are stunned. Some handle it with remarkable poise and tell their adult child, "This will take some time. But I love you—always will—and we will work through this together."

Still others tell their son or daughter, and later tell me just as genuinely, that they "don't believe in homosexuality." I tell them as respectfully as I can that their child does believe in it, which means it is a reality with which they will have to find a way to live.

Whatever their initial reaction, I have consistently been impressed with how parents put the love of their child above differences of perspective. Across the board, parents love their children profoundly and will not let anything get in the way of that love.

I will always remember the way my wife, Karen, said it, "You don't have to give up your values to stay in the relationship. Thank God, Jesus didn't." Whatever you believe, you keep your values and your integrity intact. You simply lead with grace.

8

Empty Nest

It's just the two of us on the porch again with the view as magnificent as always. It's early Sunday morning. The first light silhouettes the familiar mountain range. The fog in the valley is lighter than yesterday.

We each hold our coffee mugs with both hands. There is no breeze, but the autumn air is unusually cold. You had to go back in for a jacket.

We talk of upcoming travel plans. How many years have you two had that annual ski trip to Park City? Still doing most of the black runs. Pretty impressive. Not that I'm implying anything about your age.

You kindly ask about the first cruise we took a couple of months ago, the one to Alaska. Out comes my iPhone to show you the pictures of the whales we saw in Juneau and then the icebergs. You may regret having asked.

With the warming sun now shining on our faces, others are up, pouring their coffee and drifting out to join us. Plans for upcoming weekends become the theme. College games. A trip to New York. Golf at the coast.

You summed it up so simply, "Life is easy now. Grab the keys, and turn out the lights."

They call it the empty nest. Funny, it doesn't feel that way. No, there aren't as many of us there who call it home, but our lives are filled with the richness of friends we love, activities we value, and sons and daughters who bring us both joy and grandchildren.

The nest isn't really empty. Just transformed into something new and good.

THERE IS THE OLD STORY about the young priest and minister having lunch with the elderly rabbi. An argument breaks out among the young clergy about when life actually begins. The debate rages between whether it was the moment of conception or the moment of birth. Finally the rabbi speaks up: "You kids, you kids. You just don't understand. Life begins when the kids leave home and the dog dies."

With no disrespect to the kids or to the dog, it does begin a whole new chapter, filled with possibilities. With fewer responsibilities and more freedom, we can spread our wings in ways we could not before. We are not yet old, but we are aware there is a finish line out there, and that provides some motivation.

Finally, we turn to the last of our four goals:

*To become more focused on this new chapter of our lives;
with the nest now empty, we spread our wings, too, in new
directions with new priorities.*

We want to make the most of the rest of our lives. We want to
live intentionally. We want to invest our lives in ways that are fulfilling and have integrity for us. We want to discover directions
that give us purpose and joy. We want to have fun. We want to
give and to invest ourselves beyond ourselves. For all of us, parenting, no matter how rewarding, has drawn us away from other
meaningful activities for which we now have the freedom.

We are ready. Nothing can hold us back. Well, yes, there is
some unfinished business that can hold us back. Let me take a
moment to mention two personal issues that can burden us and
slow us down: grief and guilt. If either of these is experienced and
allowed to fester, it can dilute the richness of the lives we are
trying to develop. These emotions must be honored and taken
seriously.

A WORD ABOUT OUR SADNESS

I have mentioned regularly in the previous chapters about us letting our children go as they reach adulthood and "taking a backseat to their marriage" when they wed. This may be easily said but
not always so easily done. For many parents this is a time of real
grief. It is true this is a wonderful new beginning, but it may be a
painful ending. The loss, and its resulting grief, needs to be
mourned in whatever way has integrity for you.

After wedding services at which I officiate, I try to see certain people before the reception is over, just to touch base. They are the father of the bride and the mother of the groom. I know their tears may not just be tears of joy.

At any stage of the adult transition—graduation, a wedding, a move across country—there is the possibility for experiencing loss. First, there is the loss of the closeness of the day-to-day relationship with our children. There is also:

the loss of identity,
   the loss of our role as parent,
      the loss of "family" as we had come to know it and savor it,
         the loss of a built-in community with fellow parents.

Writer Anna Quindlen, as usual, puts it so well:

Tell me at your peril that the flight of my kids into successful adulthood is hugely liberating . . . I already had a great job into which I'd thrown myself for two decades . . . I was good at it, if I do say so myself, and because I was, I've now been demoted to part-time work. Soon I will attain emerita status. This stinks.[1]

You may well feel a similar loss and the resulting grief. Don't be embarrassed to acknowledge it. Find your way to express it, to give it a voice. I always return to the three best ways of expressing grief: cry it out, talk it out, and write it out. If you have tears, freely cry them out. If you need to talk about your sadness, have coffee with your dearest friend and let her be the friend she wants to be. If you journal, write and write and write about how you feel. All three ways will help you work through your grief and prepare you to enjoy this new place in your family.

There is a simple, but profound, dynamic behind the importance of "getting it out," of expressing your grief. Anytime something eventful happens to us, we are filled with emotional input. We are left in a place of imbalance, of emotional disequilibrium. This is true both positively and negatively, whether we receive good news or bad. So how do we right the ship? We intuitively right our imbalance from emotional *input* with emotional *output*.

What's the first thing you do with really big news—again, either good or bad—you just received? Of course, you *tell someone*. And then you tell someone else. You want to talk about it. You want to right the imbalance of the emotional input with the output of talking about it.

When you have a loss, you experience grief. That's right, you feel emotional imbalance. Get it out. Cry it out. Talk it out. Or write it out. Your ship is listing to the side. Right it, so you can now sail on.

You will stay in your previous life chapter to the degree that your grief is not expressed. Give it a voice. Grieve it, so you can let go of "what was" and embrace what now is.

THE TIMES WE REGRET

Regrets can also keep us from moving ahead. All parents have regrets. We regret the things we said and wish we could take back, and we regret the things we didn't say and wish we now could add. We regret the things we did or didn't do.

Perhaps it was an event, an isolated moment, a careless word that haunts you. Or even more painfully, it may be a pattern of yours, repeated errors as a parent that hurt your child and damaged the relationship. Or maybe it was all the ball games and recitals and swim meets that you decided to miss because there was a deal to be made or a ladder to be climbed. There are many parenting missteps we may have made:

criticizing them too much,
    not affirming them enough,
        pushing them too hard academically,
           not pushing them harder academically,

pushing them to live out our unfulfilled dreams,
    not encouraging them to discover the dreams for their lives.
        losing our temper too readily,
           not spending enough time together.

You must find your way to let go of these mistakes. You may need to talk with your children. Acknowledge what you did. Tell them what you regret. Likely it did some damage—to them personally and to your relationship with them. But wounds can heal. Please know that is true. *Wounds can heal.* Your children's wounds, properly tended, can heal. Wounds in the relationship with them, properly tended, can heal. Your acknowledgment is how the healing begins.[2]

There is another advantage to beginning this conversation. We tend to parent in the ways we were parented. By acknowledging your mistakes, you are making clear to them what you did to them is not how they should do it with their children.

Then ask for their forgiveness. Often reconciled relationships are as strong as those that never needed reconciliation. Yes, they really can be that strong. Our connection really can become strong at the broken places. If the damage was serious, if the wounds were deep, offer professional help to your children. Offer to participate with them in counseling in any way that would be useful to them, to you, and to your relationship with them. Remind them how much they mean to you and that you will do anything to help them heal.

You will also need to *forgive yourself*. Lord knows how much we love our children. We would do anything for them. Just imagining that we thoughtlessly hurt them can be a tough pill to swallow. After seeking their forgiveness, forgive yourself.

There are not many perfect parents walking around. You and I have plenty of company in the imperfect majority. Thank goodness kids are resilient. They bounce back from our mistakes. They heal as persons. We work to heal our relationships. It's time to let go of your mistakes. Leave them back there where they belong so you can live in the present and carve out a wonderful future.

I was talking with someone I had not seen in years and asked how she was doing. She said, "I'm doing really well. Now, I've still got my baggage, but at least I'm down to a *carry on*." So now, as freed of baggage as we can get—maybe even down to a carry on—we are ready to move ahead.

FIND YOUR PASSIONS

Rearing children has been a great passion. Now you are ready for others. You have the freedom to discover those for which there simply wasn't the time or energy before. Don't know where to start? Start anywhere your heart leads you, anywhere your heart tells you that you might discover real joy. If it works, *bingo*. If it's close, tweak it next time. If it bombs, you know what never to do again.

You likely have an idea where to start. There are things you always have wanted to try. Now is the time to try them. Trust your instincts. Go with your intuition. "Follow your bliss," as Joseph Campbell often said.

In an earlier chapter I noted that the traditional four life stages—childhood, adolescence, adulthood, and old age—had now been expanded to six. We focused on the new one between adolescence and adulthood called "emerging adulthood," which includes many of our adult children. The other new stage is between adulthood and old age. It's called "active retirement."[3] Many of us are in this one—or soon will be, as about 10,000 of our citizens each day are turning sixty-five.

It's the adjective in *active* retirement that is most relevant. Gone is the day when retirement was equated with passivity. We are in motion, looking for meaning, fulfillment, and enjoyment of life.

It was none other than Dolly Parton who reportedly said it best, "Find out who you are. And do it on purpose." Discover your bliss. Discover your passions. Find out what gives you joy and meaning—then do it on purpose.

My friends tell me that I am the only person they know whose brother retired *to* New York City. Not *from, to*. He retired in his midfifties from his law practice in Louisiana and a few months later called with the news that he and his wife were moving to New York City. More than a decade later, they remain as happy there—with all the plays, lectures, and readings to attend—as a couple of kids in Disney World. Follow your bliss.

Remember the book you always wanted to write? Do it now. Your memoirs—published or not—would be a wonderful gift to your family for generations to come. As clichéd as it sounds, take the course at the nearby college you had long wanted to take. No grades, no tests, no papers. Just learning for the joy of learning. Walk. Work out. Play some tennis. Read. Go to the symphony. Find your passions. Follow your bliss.

I don't know about you, but I need a purpose. I want some thing to look forward to as I get up in the morning. I don't want to *spend* the rest of my life; I want to *invest* it. I want to be intentional. I want to invest it in what I enjoy and invest it beyond me, in ways that can make a difference in others' lives. Most of the directions I take would be *purpose* with a lowercase *p*. Then there are those Purposes in my life, and in yours, that feel more like a calling. There we feel a drive, a passion, a heart-felt imperative to invest ourselves. Those directions are not ones on which we *decide* so much as we *discover*.

In what directions do you feel that sense of purpose or even Purpose? What gives your life richness and meaning? What turns you on to waking up in the morning?

A life of meaning is the result of a life that honors purpose. I want purpose, and truth be known, I'm being self-serving here. For I know that with purpose come meaning and fulfillment and joy. And I want my life to be as filled with joy as I can make it.

Be sure to spend time getting outside yourself—for your own sake. The emptiest lives I know belong to some of the most self-absorbed people. Most of us have worked hard and succeeded in achieving fulfilled lives. We are blessed. We then need to be a blessing. As I once heard it said, "If you have done well, it's your responsibility to send the elevator back down." Find your ways to give back.

And have fun. Forget meaning and purpose for a while, and do whatever you want to do just for the thrill of it. Since the movie *The Bucket List* was released, the phrase has become a frequently used addition to our vocabulary. It touched a nerve, in a positive way, in those of us who are empty nesters and are past midlife. As empty nesters, we have a newfound freedom to go and do. As those who are past midlife, we had better go and do sooner rather than later. What have you always wanted to do? What would give you a thrill? What would bring you sheer joy? If you know, start making your plans to do it. If you don't know, start making your plans to discover it. Have fun.

Oh, and spoil the grandchildren. It's in your job description.

FRIENDSHIPS

A major part of the joy in this new chapter is found in relationships. I was sitting in the kitchen of a friend's mountain cabin one Sunday morning as we all were about to pack and head back to Atlanta. (Yes, this is one of the cabins that serves as the inspiration for the preface to each chapter.) We could not have been having a better time. There must have been about a dozen of us there. Conversations erupted all over the kitchen and around the breakfast table. The consistent hum was often punctuated by a burst of laughter.

In the midst of all of this, my eyes landed on my friend who was our host. He was sitting on the far side of the room, looking at me and smiling. I read his lips as he silently mouthed the words, "It doesn't get any better than this."

Relationships. If you don't have them, develop them. If you

do have them, enjoy them. Every study I have ever read—and everyone with whom I've talked—confirms the importance of relationships to a fulfilled and meaningful life. Develop them, and enjoy them.

YOUR CHILDREN

Ellen Goodman, the columnist, wrote,

> And if the empty nest is meant to describe a family that's fledged to parts unknown, or parents who have retired from the caregiving business, it doesn't happen that way. Family does not come to an end when childhood does. There is not only a chance, but a need to rewrite the parent-child script for the next act.[4]

I was talking with our son, Patrick, last night. We were making plans for his mom's birthday party. The conversation drifted to the inevitable place: his children. Noah, who is now two, is beginning to describe his dreams when he wakes in the morning. Patrick was articulate in explaining to this little fellow what a dream is. We laughed at the fact that Noah understood exactly none of his insights. But he knew his daddy was holding him as he chatted about something. Noah knew he was loved.

This is our relationship now: father and adult son, two adults who love and respect and enjoy each other.

The talk moved back to the party. He and his wife, Pam, will be coming over this afternoon with the boys to celebrate. Little Owen will be scooting around on the den floor while Noah runs up and down his special path in our backyard. We will enjoy Patrick's delightful wit and Pam's softly spoken grace.

Our daughter, Brooke, will bring her fiancé. The two of them will stay after the others have left so we can catch up. We dearly enjoy their company. Many parents have the image that at this stage of their lives they will be dispensing their sage wisdom to these young adults. It's not that way. It's much better. It's a relationship. We learn at least as much from Brooke and Ryan as they do from us. There have been numerous tweaks and changes in this book from conversations with them.

So today we celebrate. We will have dinner; Karen will make a wish and blow out the candles. This is our family now. It is transformed. Actually, it is continually transforming. And it is a good thing.

THE OTHER GENERATION

The nest never really empties. But life is quieter now—and calmer. Books and movies, long neglected, fill more of our time. *Leisure* becomes a word with which we are reacquainted. Our pace slows. We sit back more often. We relax and unwind.

Just then the phone rings. It's your mom, now eighty-three. She asks if you could take them to Dad's doctor appointment next Tuesday. "We got turned around last time," she acknowledges. "We were embarrassed and just came back home." You get up and reach for your calendar.

Our parents are the other slice of bread for us as the sandwich generation. As we let go of one set of responsibilities, we begin to take on another. We don't complain—much. It's life. We have been on the receiving end of our parents' care and one day may well be guided by our children. But for today we are in the middle of the sandwich. Letting go and taking on. It's being family.

YOUR MARRIAGE

Many of you are married. For those who are, your spouse is the relationship I encourage you to begin developing into something deeper and more intimate. For the last twenty-something years much attention has had to be diverted away from your marriage to rear those children. Now it can get the time and attention it deserves.

Be intentional about being married. Neither you nor I have ever drifted into achieving anything worthwhile. Everything of value we ever have attained has required our being intentional. Your biggest distractions from your marriage—getting everyone to soccer practice, to piano lessons, to the tutor, and back home for dinner—have grown up and moved on.

Your marriage may have drifted farther apart than either of you realized. To your surprise, you may be living out the cliché of the couple sitting across the breakfast room table with little to say. Then get to know each other again. Spend plenty of time together. Plan it. Book it. Schedule it. Do it. Evenings at home, weekends away. Just the two of you. You are likely married to a really neat person—as is your spouse, I might add. Get to know her . . . all over again.

Or you may not have let rearing those kids get in the way of continuing to develop your relationship with each other. Congratulations. Now you can thoroughly enjoy the richness of your marriage. Make the most of this time. It may be quiet evenings or frequent trips or exciting adventures. Do together whatever brings the two of you the greatest joy.

You did it! You got 'em grown. Enjoy it.

THOSE WHO ARE SINGLE

Many who are empty nesters find themselves in a nest that may feel very empty. With the passing of the years comes death and divorce. You may now be living alone. I encourage you to be just as intentional about developing your life.

Most single empty nesters are women. Ours is a society with a large single female population. The main reason is obvious: women outlive men. Life can be lonely for them. Someone who was successfully taking medication for depression once said, "There are just no meds for loneliness." Some describe feeling like a "fifth wheel" in a largely couples world.

I talk with some who privately long for a partner in life. I hear from others who have so successfully carved out meaningful lives they "would have to think long and hard" should a potential candidate come into their lives. Either way, the key is to develop a life that maximizes one's fulfillment and joy.

I am involved with an organization in Atlanta called Women Alone Together®. (As the lone male on the board of directors, when I walk in to our meetings, I often hear, "Here comes the testosterone.") It is for women who are alone because of death, divorce, or choice. Most have adult children. Yet they are indeed alone, together. Through the book club, workshops, luncheons, and outings, their emphasis is on maximizing the enjoyment of life and doing it *together.*

I think of this group both as a resource for single women and as a metaphor for all single, empty nester adults. Make the most of your life, and enjoy much of it in relationship. Join the groups that focus on what you like to do. Engage in the activities that are fun or fulfilling for you. Surround yourself with the company of friends who give you life and energy. Develop your community. You will always have your family of origin; maintain your family of choice.

And please do one other thing. I have a friend who has been a widow for many years. Her children are long since grown. She has developed as full and meaningful a life as anyone I know. We had a long conversation once about how she had accomplished this life following her husband's death. I shall always remember her first comment: "I learned to cultivate the pleasure of my own company," she said.

She *cultivated*—isn't that the perfect word—the pleasure of being alone and engaging in the solitary activities of reading, playing the piano, gardening, or doing whatever gave her joy.

Relationships are the icing on the cake—and I do like icing on my cake—but I have to be my own cake. I have to bring a core sense of joy and fulfillment to life from within me. I have to cultivate the pleasure of my own company. The joy of the company of others is then added to the pleasure of the life I have cultivated.

GREAT FOR THE CHILDREN

As the nest empties, you, too—married or single—can spread your wings. Take on new interests and directions, or pursue familiar paths. Take off the shelf those pursuits you wanted to get to with your friends or life partners when you "had the time" or those activities you engage in alone.

This is good for us and *great for our children*. If we move on with our lives, we both get out of their way and position ourselves perfectly for the very best relationship with them. As we move ahead and fully reside in this new chapter, we will not be hanging on to the old habit of hands-on parenting, which is no good for anyone.

I have many young adult friends. Some are friends of my son and daughter. Others are sons and daughters of my friends. Many are fellow members of my church. I have talked with most of them—led discussions in a couple of their Sunday school classes—about the ideas in this book to get their valuable feedback. These young adults invariably smile when I ask about their parents "moving on" after they leave.

They have moved on and want their parents to do the same. That was then, and this is now. They couldn't care less that their parents had reclaimed and redecorated their old rooms—"Thank goodness," one said—or even sold the house and downsized. They want us to move on in every sense and enjoy our lives thoroughly.

Now. Now is the time. Now is your time. Claim who you are at this moment, in this new chapter with its freedoms and possibilities. Claim it, and then live it.

Epilogue

OUR CHILDREN ARE BORN into our care totally dependent on us. They turn to us for every need. This begins their journey toward independence. Step by step, day by day, they develop the ability, the language, the skills, and the maturity of living independently as adults.

We, in turn, bit by bit release them to be in charge of their lives. We begin letting go—in small ways to start. We let go of their hand as they take those early steps, of the bicycle as they steer down the driveway, of the car keys as we tell them to drive safely. We say good-bye as they nervously close the car door for their first day of school, as they wave to us from outside their freshman dorm, as they rush hand-in-hand to the limo to head off on their honeymoon.

We let go. There is ample nostalgia, but we now relax, and we feel a faint smile come across our lips.

Job well done.

Notes

1. Letting Go

1. My thanks to Alyce McKenzie who inspired these opening vignettes in her book *Novel Preaching*.

2. I am grateful to Jap Keith for this beautiful note sent to us after the birth of our son, Patrick.

3. As quoted in Karen Stabiner, *The Empty Nest* (New York: Voice, 2007), 274–75.

2. Today's Young Adults

1. "Bring on the Learning Revolution!" Sir Ken Robinson speech at TED Conference, Long Beach, California, February 2010; www.ted.com/talks/sir_ken_robinson_bring_on_the_revolution.html (accessed 4 September 2011).

2. Randall Stross, "The Wristwatch Is Reimagined: Will Young Shoppers Care?" *New York Times*, 19 March 2011; www.nytimes.com /2010/03/20/business/20digi.html?_r=1&scp=1&sq=The+wristwatch+ is+reimagined++Stross&st=nyt.

3. Ross Campbell and Gary Chapman, *Parenting Your Adult Child* (Chicago: Northfield Publishing, 1999), 17.

4. "The Greatest Man I Never Knew," by Richard Leigh and Layng Martine Jr. © 1992 MCA Records. When I cite songs, I include the songwriter(s), copyright dates, and publishing companies; this information is usually found in the liner notes.

5. Campbell and Chapman, *Parenting*, 15–16.

6. Ibid., 17, 20.

7. Bruce Tulgan, *Not Everyone Gets a Trophy* (San Francisco: Jossey-Bass, 2009), 7.

8. "How Young People View Their Lives, Futures and Politics," Pew Research Center, 9 January 2007, 5–6.

9. Neil Howe and William Strauss, *Millennials Rising* (New York: Vintage Books, 2000), 8–9.

10. Tulgan, *Trophy*, 13.

11. Ibid., 10–11.

12. "How Young People View Their Lives," 2.

13. Ibid., 20, 23.

14. Jean Twenge and W. Keith Campbell, *The Narcissism Epidemic* (New York: Free Press, 2009), 16.

15. Ibid., 73.

16. Ibid., 30.

17. "How Young People View Their Lives," 18.

18. Tulgan, *Trophy*, 14.

19. Jeffrey Jensen Arnett, *Emerging Adulthood* (New York: Oxford University Press, 2004), 51, 70.

3. Resetting the Sails

1. Robin Marantz Henig, "What Is It about 20-Somethings?" *New York Times*, 18 August 2010; www.nytimes.com/2010/08/22/magazine/22Adulthood-t.html (accessed 3 September 2011).

2. David Brooks, *The Social Animal* (New York: Random House, 2011), 190.

3. Jeffrey Jensen Arnett, *Emerging Adulthood* (New York: Oxford University Press, 2004), 15.

4. Ruth Nemzoff, *Don't Bite Your Tongue* (New York: Palgrave Macmillan, 2008), 52.

5. Lewis Grizzard, *My Daddy Was a Pistol and I'm a Son of a Gun* (New York: Villard Books, 1986). Quotation used by permission of the estate of Lewis Grizzard. www.lewisgrizzard.com.

6. Thomas A. Harris, *I'm OK—You're OK* (New York: Harper & Row, 1967), 16–36.

7. Barbara Kantrowitz, "The Fine Art of Letting Go," *Newsweek*, 22 May 2006; http://www.newsweek.com/2006/05/21/the-fine-art-of-letting-go.html.

8. "Story Corps Celebrates Moms, This Time in Print," National Public Radio, 8 May 2010; www/npr.org/templates/transcript/transcript.php?storyId=126622735.

9. Stephen Covey, *The Seven Habits of Highly Effective People* (New York: Simon & Schuster, 1989), 239.

4. Respecting Their Need for Respect

1. Ruth Nemzoff, *Don't Bite Your Tongue* (New York: Palgrave Macmillan, 2008), 53.

2. Thomas A. Harris, *I'm OK—You're OK* (New York: Harper & Row, 1967), 18–28.

5. Good-bye, Hello

1. Robin Marantz Henig, "What Is It about 20-Somethings?" *New York Times*, 18 August 2010; www.nytimes.com/2010/08/22/magazine/22Adulthood-t.html (accessed 3 September 2011).

2. Jeffrey Jensen Arnett, *Emerging Adulthood* (New York: Oxford University Press, 2004), 21–24.

3. David Brooks, *The Social Animal* (New York: Random House, 2011), 190.

4. Arnett, *Emerging Adulthood*, 8.

5. Michael J. Rosenfeld, "The Independence of Young Adults," *Family Therapy Magazine*, May/June 2010, 18.

6. Ibid.

7. Martha Straus, "Bungee Families," *Psychotherapy Networker,* September/October 2009, 30.

8. Robert Frost, "The Death of the Hired Man," in *North of Boston* (New York: Henry Holt & Co., 1915).

9. Straus, "Bungee Families," 33.

10. Arnett, *Emerging Adulthood,* 70–71.

11. Brad Sachs, "Foot on the Gas, Foot on the Brake," *Psychotherapy Networker,* September/October 2009, 59.

12. Jane Bryant Quinn, "All in the Family," *AARP Bulletin,* January/February 2011, 22.

13. Dan Kadlec, "Write Your Kids Off (On Your Taxes)," *Time,* 2 May 2011; www.time.com/time/specials/packages/article/0,28804, 2069211_2069210_2069189,00.html.

14. Ron Lieber, "When the Fledglings Return to the Nest," *New York Times,* 11 July 2009; www.nytimes.com/2009/07/11/your-money/household-budgeting/11money.html.

15. Sachs, "Foot on the Gas," 40.

16. Ibid., 42.

17. Straus, "Bungee Families," 34.

18. Barry van Gerbig, "The Truth Teller," *Sports Illustrated,* 15 June 2009, 60–61.

6. Supporting Their New Lives

1. David Brooks, *The Social Animal* (New York: Random House, 2011), 190.

2. Jeffrey Jensen Arnett, *Emerging Adulthood* (New York: Oxford University Press, 2004), 97–100.

3. Catherine Rampell, "Many with New College Degree Find the Job Market Humbling," *New York Times*, 18 May 2011; www.nytimes.com/2011/05/19/business/economy/19grads.html?_r=1&scp=1&sq=Many%20with%20new%20college%20degree%20find%20the%20job%20market%20humbling&st=cse.

4. Dan Kadlec, "Write Your Kids Off (On Your Taxes)," *Time*, 2 May 2011; www.time.com/time/specials/packages/article/0,28804,2069211_2069210_2069189,00.html.

5. Ibid.

7. Dealing with the Difficult Times

1. "What Are the Signs and Symptoms of Depression?" National Institute of Mental Health; www.nimh.nih.gov/health/publications/depression/what-are-the-signs-and-symptoms-of-depression.shtml (accessed 3 September 2011).

2. "Developmental Disabilities: Topic Home," Centers for Disease Control and Prevention; www.cdc.gov/ncbddd/dd/ (accessed 3 September 2011).

8. Empty Nest

1. Anna Quindlen, "Flown Away, Left Behind," *Newsweek*, 11 January 2004.

2. Jeanette C. Lauer and Robert H. Lauer, *How to Survive and Thrive in an Empty Nest* (Oakland, Calif.: New Harbinger Publications, 1999), 74–75.

3. David Brooks, *The Social Animal* (New York: Random House, 2011), 190.

4. As quoted in Karen Stabiner, *The Empty Nest* (New York: Voice, 2007), 280.

Also by Ronald J. Greer

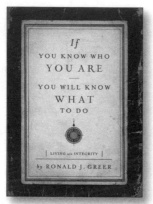

A timely look at the importance
of integrity
ISBN 978-1-4267-4461-7

A message about hope and fulfillment,
for those who are mourning
ISBN 978-0-687-33363-9

"The closing sentence of this book says it all. 'I look up, and I am reminded to be all that I was created to be.' And all the other preceding sentences are a wise and very pastoral guide to the life-affirming art of learning to do just that—to look up and be all that we are created to be."
—Phyllis Tickle, author of *The Great Emergence*

Integrity means doing the right thing when we know it's the right thing to do. It means knowing who we are, and then being true to the lives to which we have been called. Integrity is about how we live our lives, both when someone's watching and when there is not a soul in sight.

Drawing on his experience as a Christian, minister, and pastoral counselor, Ronald J. Greer explores the two sides of integrity: personal integrity and moral integrity. Personal integrity involves an integrated life where we are in harmony with ourselves. Moral integrity reflects the idea of morality and ethics merged with the concept of wholeness.

Perfect for the graduate or as a gift for anyone at a key turning point in life, this small book provides insight and guidelines that will become touchstones for a good, well-lived life.

This book includes a discussion guide.

AVAILABLE WHEREVER FINE BOOKS ARE SOLD.